DAY-BY-DAY

A Program of Preparation for Christian Marriage

by
John J. Colligan and Kathleen A. Colligan
with
The Broome County Council Of Churches

PAULIST PRESS
New York/Mahwah, N.J.

ISBN: 0-8091-3457-8

Published by Paulist Press
997 Macarthur Boulevard
Mahwah, New Jersey 07430

Printed and bound in the
United States of America

Contents

Acknowledgments

We are deeply indebted to the Family Life Committee of the Broome County Council of Churches for their initiation of this project and diligent shepherding of its progress. We especially thank Rev. Mark Ridley, Rev. Douglas Sivers, Msgr. Peter Owens, and Rev. William Stanton for the many hours they devoted to directing our efforts. We thank the Hoyt and Decker Foundations for their support of this development. For the past twenty years we have been enriched by the insights about Christian marriage taught by Fr. Chuck Gallagher, S.J., and we thank him for loving the body of Christ in such a passionate way.

The DAY-BY-DAY Symbol...

In the center are your intertwined wedding rings, a sign of your oneness as a couple. Woven through the rings is a dogwood branch. Legend tells us that Jesus was hung on a cross made of dogwood. So the cross of Jesus blesses our Christian marriage. The dogwood is an early spring sign of new life to the world. Your marriage is a sign of new life to the Christian church. When the blossoms fade and fall, the dogwood leaves remain green. When the memories of your courtship fade in time, the beauty of your on-going love for each other is a witness of Christ's love for his church.

This book is called DAY-BY-DAY as a reminder that your wedding day is only the first day of your Christian marriage, and that your love will grow for each other DAY-BY-DAY.

This symbol was designed and executed by William Mihalko, a Johnson City, N.Y. artist and teacher who has worked extensively with religious symbolism.

What Is DAY-BY-DAY?

DAY-BY-DAY is a program designed for use by all Christian denominations. It focuses on basic Christian teachings about married love: that the couple develop an intimate level of trust in communication, grow toward a mature sexuality, and develop a spirituality based on the scriptural teachings of Jesus.

The DAY-BY-DAY program and the book contain a series of teachings and exercises designed to help engaged couples listen to and understand one another on an ever deeper level. It is not meant to take the place of the pastor's discussions with the engaged, but to supplement what each member of the clergy would like his/her couples to know before marriage, using members of the congregation as part of the team.

DAY-BY-DAY can be used in a variety of settings, from an ordinary living room to a large church hall. It can be used as a one day program (8:30 a.m.—6:00 p.m.) or as a series of four two-hour sessions. It can be done by a team couple working one-on-one with the engaged or be part of a team effort that would include two team couples and possibly a member of the clergy if available. It has been done with mixed groups of couples representing a variety of religious denominations as well as with couples who are all part of the same denomination.

The outlines are easy to use and involve minimal preparation time. Included in each session are: prayer, scripture, teaching, and written exercises for the engaged couples to answer and share privately with one another. The outlines include Catholic inserts where appropriate. All scripture quotes are taken from *New Oxford Annotated Bible*, edited by Bruce Metzger and Roland E. Murphy, Oxford University Press, New York, 1991. Any good modern translation may be substituted.

The DAY-BY-DAY book can be offered as a take-home book to the engaged or be used by the pastor or the marriage preparation team to work individually with the couple. The book is appropriate as a take-home for all engaged couples regardless of the marriage preparation program used.

The Role of the Pastor

The pastor's role is central to any marriage preparation—so central that no program, including this one, would exist without the involvement of caring ministers who want to offer their engaged couples the best preparation possible for marriage.

Essentially, each pastor who is part of the program *will do much that has always been done, only now there will be help.* The engaged will make the initial contact with their pastor to inquire about having their wedding at church. There will follow at least one meeting to get to know the couple and their plans and to establish any requirements the congregation asks of the engaged couple as they enter into marriage.

In addition to the DAY-BY-DAY workshop, we recommend that the pastor or a person/couple delegated by the pastor administer any of the following *standardized tests* to the engaged:

1. *Myers-Briggs Type Indicator* or *Keirsey Bates Type Indicator.* Keirsey Bates is similar to Myers-Briggs but has a shorter questionnaire. Keirsey Bates also does not require you to be certified in order to administer it. Both programs give couples some idea of their own personality type as well as the type of their future spouses. The book *Please Understand Me* explains a great deal about personality types, and a manual, *Using Type with Couples*, further enhances the opportunity to help couples understand their strengths and weaknesses. All materials may be ordered from:

   > Type Resources, Inc.
   > 101 Chestnut St. #135
   > Gaithersburg, MD 20877
   > (303) 963-1283 or (800) 456-6284

2. *Pre-Marriage Inventories.* Several are available on the market. They are a series of questions designed to clarify points of agreement and disagreement for the engaged couple. It's a great help to the pastor to know the couple better and offer them guidance in the specific areas targeted by the inventory. It also enables couples to understand better what their partners are thinking and opens doors to communication. Inventories cover such topics as: finances, in-laws, communications, religion, children, sex and sexuality, readiness for marriage, extended family, etc.

Two well-tested programs are:

FOCCUS
Family Life Office
3214 N. 60th St.
Omaha, NE 68104
(402) 551-9003

PREPARE/ENRICH
P.O. Box 190
Minneapolis, MN 55440
(612) 331-1661

Choosing the Marriage Preparation Team

The pastor may wish to participate in the DAY-BY-DAY workshop and may, in fact, be a regular part of the team. If it's impossible for the pastor to be present, then it's always desirable for him/her to be there at the beginning of the day to introduce the team and assure the engaged couples of support from the church. Also, if a closing celebration is planned, a member of the clergy will want to be present for prayers and/or a special blessing for the engaged couples. If you are clustering with a number of other churches to present DAY-BY-DAY, it is only necessary to have one clergy member present from the entire group.

The pastor should choose a number of married couples from the congregation who will form the basic marriage preparation team. The couples should be chosen in prayer. They may be of any age, but we recommend some younger as well as a few older couples.

They should be *the people who stand out in your mind for their faithfulness to one another and to God and their desire to live a strong Christian marriage. They don't need to have a perfect marriage* in the sense that they never fight and everything is always wonderful. However, they *should be capable of sharing* themselves and their experiences with others. This will call for a great deal of honesty and humility. The most powerful thing they will portray is their love—for one another, for God, and for the engaged couples. The couples you invite to be on the presenting team for DAY-BY-DAY will discover that they will get a lot more out of it than the engaged couples, because they will be much more aware of the quality of loving in their own relationship on a daily basis. (A sample copy of a letter from the pastor to prospective team couples is offered later in this chapter.)

The easiest way to train a potential team couple to present DAY-BY-DAY is to invite them to attend a DAY-BY-DAY workshop offered nearby. If this isn't possible, simply gather the team together and go over the materials as a group. They can divide the talks according to who feels most comfortable with each topic.

Understanding the Material

Whether or not the pastor is part of the DAY-BY-DAY team, it's a good idea for him/her to at least be familiar with the material covered in the program. *There are three major topics included: Communications, Gift of Sexuality, and Covenant of Marriage.* The workshop is *designed to enhance the communications skills of the couples* and to enable them to go deeper into their own relationship. The focus of the workshop is on developing a more positive attitude about the meaning of Christian marriage; it is not a problem-solving experience.

Meet with the Engaged

There is no way any marriage preparation program can adequately cover all that can and should be said. (Even if you can say it all, engaged couples are often not ready to listen.) Therefore, *the engaged couples should receive a DAY-BY-DAY book of take-home exercises* at the end of their DAY-BY-DAY workshop. Even if the couples do not attend the workshop, *the book summarizes all the topics covered in the program as well as a variety of other important subjects such as finances, in-laws, criticism, arguments, and roles of men and women.* You may wish to use some of these exercises from the book when you individually counsel some of your engaged couples, especially if you see a special need.

During the DAY-BY-DAY workshop the engaged will also receive a brief document that will discuss when a marriage should be postponed. This may offer you a further opportunity to discuss a delicate matter with the engaged couple, especially if there are doubts about their readiness for marriage. A copy of this document is printed at the end of this chapter, and is also included in the set of Exercise handouts.

It is always worthwhile to spend time with the engaged couple after the workshop at a *follow-up meeting*. In this way, you can get feedback about what the couple has learned and also answer any questions they may have. Throughout the day at the workshop, the couples are encouraged to turn to their pastor as a source of guidance and direction both before and after marriage.

Meeting with the couple also allows the pastor *to clarify the teachings of the church on certain issues and to provide the couple with any books or booklets you may wish to make available to them.* There is always a need for good Christian materials clarifying a healthy perspective on life. Additionally, there are always couples who have practiced chastity and would benefit from good Christian material about married love. Even those who are more sexually experienced would find such books helpful.

Involving the Congregation

In order to make the engaged couple more at home in the faith community, it is often a good idea to *include the congregation in a supportive role.*

Some congregations provide *prayer partners* for the engaged couple, to pray for the couple throughout their time of preparation. They may *write the engaged couple a love letter* just before their marriage or they may wish to *invite the engaged couple to their home* after the DAY-BY-DAY workshop.

Some congregations wish to *acknowledge their engaged at a regular Sunday service* by either bringing them forward for a blessing or having a betrothal ceremony. Each denomination has its own traditions and each faith community has a different charism. We suggest you do whatever is appropriate for your community at the time.

We are personally grateful to the pastors of all denominations who have enriched our lives and enabled us to prepare this program. It is our hope that it will enable you to minister more easily to engaged couples and that it will inspire them to desire to live a great Christian marriage.

[Sample letter to be sent by the pastor to prospective team couples for the DAY-BY-DAY workshops]

[Date]

Dear Ralph and Sally,

As a pastor, it's important to me to offer our engaged couples the best marriage preparation possible. When I look at the current divorce statistics (47-50% of all marriages will end in divorce), I realize the seriousness of the need to help couples prepare for marriage and give them the tools necessary to live a lifelong marriage commitment.

Since we've met, I've been aware of your love for each other and your love for God. (*Mention any specific qualities you see in the couple such as: sense of humor, gentleness with each other, affection for each other, devotion to family, etc.*) You have built your life together on faith, and I believe you are an outstanding role model for Christian marriage. As your pastor, I'd like to recognize your efforts, and as your friend, I'm asking you to spend the gifts God has given you for others.

This (*fall, spring, etc.*) we'll be starting a new marriage preparation program called DAY-BY-DAY. The presenting team consists of one member of the clergy and several married couples. It's a program that is relatively easy to present and does not require a great deal of writing or advance preparation. It's not necessary to have a professional degree in education or counseling to present the program.

It would require a few team meetings to prepare your presentations and some degree of honesty and humility to share your own experiences in marriage. The teaching is all written out ahead of time. You would only have to fill in with your own personal examples to illustrate each point.

I'm inviting both of you to come to a meeting on (*date and time*) at (*place*) to meet the rest of the team and look over the materials for DAY-BY-DAY. Coming to the meeting will in no way obligate you to be part of the team if you should choose not to be involved but should help you make an informed decision.

Since this is a serious commitment, I'm asking you to pray about this before you give me your final answer. If you have any questions or if you can't make the meeting, please let me know. Otherwise, I'll be expecting you.

In Christ's love,

(Pastor's signature)

When To Consider Postponing the Wedding

Postponing a wedding is always considered a drastic alternative—so drastic that few people consider it. However, there are times when postponement may be the kindest and most intelligent thing to do. Here are some ideas to keep in mind if you should be having any doubts at all about whether or not you should marry.

When Should You Consider Postponing the Wedding?

- If either of you is basically an unhappy person—and only you can make the other happy.
- If either of you drinks too much or gets drunk frequently.
- If friends and family, job or hobbies are a higher priority than you are to each other.
- If either of you takes drugs.
- If either of you feels forced into marriage.
- If either of you has serious psychological difficulties and refuses to get help.
- If either of you has serious doubts about marrying but believes in going ahead because you made a commitment to one another.
- If either of you is trying to escape an unhappy home or difficult living situation.
- If either of you is marrying for money or financial security.
- If either of you is rebounding from a previous relationship.
- If either of you is marrying to prove something to others.
- If either of you has doubts about marrying the other but is reluctant to start over with someone new.
- If either of you is afraid you'll never marry anyone if you pass up this opportunity.
- If either of you feels as if you're settling for someone less than you wanted.
- If either of you is marrying because you don't want to upset the other person or your families by postponing the wedding or breaking the engagement.
- If either of you simply believes that one or both of you are not ready for marriage.
- If either of you refuses to change and takes the position, "What you see is what you get."

Don't marry anyone to rescue him/her. If you love one another, get help first. Go for counseling or treatment. After treatment is successfully completed, plan your wedding.

If you are pregnant, and are getting married because of the pregnancy, consider postponing the wedding until several months after the baby is born. The best gift you can give your baby is parents who truly love each other and chose to be married because they wanted to be together forever. The decision to marry should be made in complete freedom. You never want to say to one another in the future, "I wouldn't have married you if it weren't for that kid!"

If you have been unable to communicate well today—if you refuse to listen to each other seriously or to speak honestly to each other—communications won't become easier over time, only more difficult. You may want to take advantage of a few sessions with a professional counselor to help you in your communication skills.

You are about to take one of the most important steps in your life—perhaps the most important step. You are choosing to make a lifelong commitment to one other person—a person who will be with you through all the seasons of your life, all the way until death.

The only reason to marry is because you have found the most wonderful person in the world for you. You are deeply, passionately in love and you cannot imagine life without one another. You have found someone you can grow and share with physically, mentally, and spiritually. You share an outlook on life that draws you closer together and to God. Life doesn't get any better than this! Go for it!

The Role of the Presenting Team

1. Advance Preparation

The DAY-BY-DAY workshop for marriage preparation is relatively easy to present. However, if you have never done this type of thing before, you may have many questions about how to proceed. We'll summarize everything you need to know in the following remarks. If you have any further questions, you should consult with your pastor or call the authors directly—(607) 748-4743.

A. Prepare Yourself

The most important part of the preparation for the day is not the work you'll do on your talks. *The most important thing is who you are*—a couple who deeply love one another and God and are actively working on your own marriage. Your most effective message will be in sharing yourselves and your relationship.

By this, we don't mean that you must have a perfect marriage, but you should be investing yourselves every day in growing closer in oneness. You must be committed to learning more about what a Christian marriage is and how to communicate with each other more effectively. Based on our experience in giving talks as a married couple, no matter what you are teaching in your talk, the audience will always observe the quality of your relationship. Just be real and share the story of your love.

If you find that during the days and weeks before the program you're having difficulties with one another, you may also share that with the couples. Just be sure to include the fact that you are determined to work out the difficulty. (For example: We were presenting talks to the engaged a few years ago over a series of six evenings. One evening we were having a serious argument over something that had come up in the family. We apologized to the couples when they came in and told them about our disagreement. As objective third parties, they could see both sides of the argument, and they added their own comments. The following week, when they returned, the first ques-

10

tion they asked before we began was, "How did it all turn out? Who won?" We were able to explain how we solved the dilemma with no winners and no losers. We both won.)

You don't have to be dishonest with the couples and pretend you have the perfect marriage. You should simply be yourselves. Be real. Allowing the couples to see you as ordinary people who love each other even when times are difficult gives them hope for their own relationship, which will certainly know at least a few hard times.

The success of the program has much to do with your own attitude toward marriage—whether or not you believe in it and value it—as well as your attitude toward the couples who come to the church for their marriage ceremony.

B. Attitudes Toward the Engaged

If those who work with the engaged couples are cynical or hostile about the future happiness of the couples, believing they are only using the church to satisfy the wishes of their parents or so they can have an attractive setting for their wedding, these attitudes will come through.

Even if your assumptions are correct, *pray that God will free you of your judgments* so that you may truly transmit to the couples the love God has for them and his desire to be intimately involved in their lives.

Marriage preparation is a wonderful opportunity to give witness to our Christian faith:

1. To make the Lord real and present to someone who may not believe in God.
2. To reveal the level of love within the faith community to those who may not have had the opportunity to be part of a religious congregation or who have been inactive.
3. To affirm the believing Christian in the decision to come to the church for marriage.

C. Typical Concerns of Those Asked To Be Team Members

Sometimes team couples are uncomfortable about discussing Christian marriage with other couples. Some believe they aren't worthy of such a mission. Yet, you were asked by your pastor to do this important work because the people of your congregation saw something special in you.

You may say to yourself, "Well, if they lived with us for a few weeks, they wouldn't think so highly of us." That's not likely. Every couple has differences of opinion and difficult times in marriage. *What your church members saw in you was your incredible love for one another through good times and bad, your overall commitment to one another, your ability to forgive and go on in your relationship, your love for God and faithfulness to God's call.*

Some protest that they are not gifted teachers, and that therefore they should not be part of the team. *Your non-verbal witness is far more important than anything you will say.* The fact that you care enough about one another and the couples to volunteer your time to encourage and support them as they prepare for their marriage speaks loudly of the love that is within you.

Sometimes *the most powerful witnesses are those who are simple, ordinary people,* who tell their own story in the most direct way. (Jesus did not reveal his teaching to the learned and the clever, but to the simple.) Look at the people he chose to be his apostles and disciples, the ones he trusted to tell his story. Your Christian marriage is part of his story, and you have been invited to share it with these engaged couples. Be assured that the outlines in the Leaders' Guide contain all the teaching that is needed; you simply add your story.

Essentially what you are being asked to do is to *relate to the engaged couples as if they were part of your family.* If you were to sit down with your brother and sister over a cup of coffee, what are all the things you would like to tell them about how they can best live out their Christian marriage relationship?

Some protest that they cannot do this because they are *not professionals* in counseling. We live in a society that is heavily dependent on professionals and experts. But *you are the expert on your own marriage and your own relationship.* That is what you are asked to share. If you discover that any of the engaged you are working with have serious problems and need the help of an expert, be sure to discuss this with your own pastor or the member of the clergy who is on the team so that an appropriate referral may be made.

D. Broken Engagements Postponed Marriages

An important challenge to those who work in marriage preparation is the possibility of a broken engagement. Any effective marriage preparation program will result in postponed weddings or a broken engagement from time to time.

The purpose of the courtship period is to allow the dating couple to gather data about one another and one another's families. Often, in our culture, this data-gathering is short-changed, particularly if the couple has become sexually involved with one another at an early stage in their courtship. The tendency, then, is to put data-gathering on hold and to simply enjoy the moment.

When the couple begins to plan a lifetime together, however, *it's appropriate and necessary to take a second long look at one another,* to ask the questions: "Is this someone I will only enjoy for today, or is this someone I can spend 50, 60, 70 years of my life with? Is this a family I can marry into, or are there basic problems that will never be resolved? Can the two of us handle the problems on our own?"

Couples who live together before marriage are a particular challenge because they often arrive with a certain amount of hostility and defensiveness. They believe (correctly) that the church community does not approve of their living arrangement, and they're hostile because they believe that they already have shown they can be happily married. They have tried it out with one another.

As the presenting team, it's important to keep a few facts in mind. The *divorce rate for first-time marriages hovers at about 50%. For those who have lived together before marriage, the divorce rate is higher.* Those who have lived together often have a more difficult time adjusting after marriage than those who have not. Their expectations of one another have changed. Often what was acceptable before marriage is no longer very tolerable in the light of a lifelong commitment. All the engaged need you and what you have to say even if they don't appreciate it at the moment.

Undoubtedly, you will also have *some participants who have been previously married and who will tell you they know all about marriage.* It may be true that they're experts on their previous marriage, but they are not experts on the marriage they are about to enter into. This is a new relationship and a new family they are forming; it deserves their best efforts.

A broken engagement is always a wrenching experience. If you believe you were a part of it by something you said during a presentation, you may feel responsible or guilty. But the ultimate decision about whether to marry is made by the couple themselves. Although at the time it seems like a tragedy, it would be far more tragic years later, after promises have been made and children have arrived, if the couple decides to divorce.

A broken engagement is a rare occurrence. When it happens, trust that God was present and gave the couple insight into a difference that was simply too big to ignore and impossible to overcome.

E. Concerns of the Engaged

Engaged couples have many thoughts which are part of the *hidden agenda of marriage preparation.* They are usually not mentioned because the couple is trying to put their best foot forward with the presenting team. No matter how often you assure them that the day is not a test to see if they can get married, they won't be really certain of that until the day is almost over and they have come to trust you.

It's helpful, therefore, to keep a few thoughts in mind as you deal with the engaged that will help you understand and be more compassionate with them—especially if they seem distant or hostile on arrival.

1. *Some engaged couples come fearing that you'll lecture them about how they should live as married couples.* Only they can decide how they will live out their marriage. Every relationship is unique. You'll only be offering insights into marriage and sharing a few of your own experiences. What they do with that information is up to them.

2. *Others arrive fearing a broken engagement.* "If he/she knew the real me,

would he/she still want to marry me?" Others will say, "Look, I've invested all this time into this relationship. I know he/she is not perfect, but I'm not about to break up with him/her and start over with someone else." Often they will marry, even though it's obvious to everyone around them that, at best, it will be a difficult marriage. No one on the team, however, is going to tell them whether or not they can marry. If there is a serious problem, be sure to let their pastor know about it so it can be addressed before the wedding.

3. *Some believe that any spouse is better than no spouse at all.* Some are acutely aware of their age and believe that time is running out for them. Both men and women might be concerned about the "biological clock." Women worry that they won't be able to conceive after a certain age; men worry that they will be old fathers with young children.

4. *If there is a pregnancy involved, the couple may experience a special urgency to be married* and "do the right thing" or "give the baby a name."

As a team, it's important to remember that the work of the day is in the hands of God. The outline for each talk includes a prayer at the beginning to ask God to lift these and all the barriers each one brings to the experience so that both the team and the participants will be open to the work of the Holy Spirit.

2. Preparing for the Workshop

A. Registration

There should be a contact person (or couple) in charge of registration. After the engaged couple talks with their pastor, doing the preliminary work of preparation for marriage, they should call the contact person to register for the marriage preparation workshop. It's best if the engaged handle the registration themselves, allowing them to assume responsibility for their presence that day. This also allows the contact person to answer any questions they may have about the program.

The contact person can be a church secretary, a member of the DAY-BY-DAY team, or a volunteer from the congregation or group of churches who are sponsoring the day. You only need one contact person. *The responsibilities of the contact person are:*

1. *Keep a roster of all who register for the program.* The roster should include the names of the couples and the pastor who will witness their wedding, their addresses, phone numbers, church, and the date of their wedding.

2. About ten days before the workshop, the contact person should *mail a letter to all who have registered,* welcoming them, reminding them of the

date, place (with directions if necessary) and time schedule for the day, plus any other information that may be necessary. (There is a sample letter at the end of this chapter.)

3. It is helpful if the contact person also *sends the roster to each pastor who has couples registered* for the program, circling the names of the couples from that congregation.

4. Each of the *team couples and clergy on the team should also receive a copy of the roster* so they know how many to expect at the workshop, and can begin praying for each of the engaged couples.

5. The contact person should also *maintain a list of the names of all the team members* along with their addresses, phone numbers, church affiliation, and which talks they have prepared. In this way, when a new team is being formed or a substitute is needed, all the necessary information is quickly available.

6. The contact person should keep *a list of any of the engaged couples who may be chosen as future team members* after they have been married about a year or two. The contact person may also handle all money collected from the workshop and be responsible for paying the bills and distributing printed material and other supplies to the team. The amended roster, all money collected, and remainder of supplies should be returned to the sponsoring office on the first workday after the workshop.

B. Cost of the Workshop

The *cost of the DAY-BY-DAY workshop will vary,* depending on the locale and extra expenses anticipated by the local community. It is recommended that the engaged couples be asked to bear all of this cost, unless the local congregation wishes to pay, or the couple is unable to pay, in which case exemption should be granted. A $10 fee at the time of registration is recommended, with the remainder to be paid as the couples arrive for the workshop.

Since costs do vary, each locale should consider what their actual expenses will be and set their own fee for the workshop. Some things to consider are:

1. Fee for room rental and janitorial service.

2. Cost of refreshments provided. (Coffee, tea, soft drinks or other cold beverage. Possibly doughnuts for the morning. Also a simple lunch is suggested.)

3. Cost of materials for the team and participants. (Pens, name tags, Leaders' Guides for team, copies of each exercise for each participant, and take-home books.)

4. Any extra costs you wish to assume. (Baby-sitting for children of team members, a dinner to close the day, a gift or token of the day for the engaged, etc.)

C. Gathering the Team

The team couples should be chosen by the pastor and the local congregation. Each team couple and each member of the clergy should receive a copy of the Leaders' Guide and the take-home book.

A general meeting for all team members in the area can be held once or twice a year to introduce new team members to the program and to help experienced team members write new talks and go through the mechanics of the program with those who are inexperienced.

The team for each DAY-BY-DAY workshop should consist of two or three married couples and at least one member of the clergy. How frequently team members present the program will depend on their availability and willingness to set aside the time. It's suggested that the team consist of at least one younger couple and one more experienced couple in marriage. This, however, is not always possible, and each local community should decide how they will proceed.

Once a team has been chosen for a workshop and has a specific date in mind, they should *invite one couple to be the team leaders for that workshop.* This couple will make sure that all the talk assignments are made for the workshop, and will set dates for a series of meetings for the teams to go over the talks and read their sharings. In this way, the team members will get to be comfortable with one another and with the material they'll be presenting.

The team leaders will also take care of the details of the workshop and make sure arrangements are made for the place, food, participants materials, etc. In some locales a separate committee can be set up to handle these matters, or teams who are not presenting at that workshop may wish to help out.

A *suggested format for two team meetings* before the workshop:

1. *First Team Meeting.* Team members read aloud the first three talks to the whole team to ensure that they clearly cover the outline and are of proper time length.

2. *Second Team Meeting.* The remainder of the talks are read aloud and all administrative details for the workshop are finalized (time to arrive, who will handle registration at the door, who will handle beverages, who will handle food, who will set up the room and clean up, who will be timekeeper for the day to make sure it all flows smoothly, who will bring a Bible that day, etc.).

Plan to stay an extra 10-15 minutes on the day of the workshop to note how the workshop went, to make suggestions for improving the next one, and to identify which of the engaged couples might eventually make good team members for a future workshop.

The team leaders should pass on this information to the contact person, along with the money collected and bills to be paid, and any surplus materials.

D. Preparing the Talks

Keep them simple. Share yourself. Give clear, concise examples to illustrate the point you are trying to make. The places for personal examples are clearly marked in some places in the outline. However, *you may add your own examples anywhere you wish.* The important thing is that *the examples you use should illustrate the point you're making and should be brief.* The *maximum* time allowed for each talk is marked in the schedule.

It's important to remember that the day is for the engaged couples and they need the maximum amount of time to share with one another. Even then, they will sometimes find themselves rushed to finish. Give them as much time as possible.

Stick to the Outline. Read the teaching directly from the outline in an "off-the-page" style, i.e. have as much eye contact with your audience as possible. If you're nervous, tell them so. They'll understand. There are many notes to the team distributed throughout the outlines; you do *not* read these to the engaged couples.

Feel free to write all over the outlines. You may wish to divide up the parts of the talk ahead of time. *Only one couple should present each talk.* Since there are no parts specifically set aside for the clergy, decide who is going to say which part, and mark your initials clearly in the margin of the outline. The pastor on the team might decide to share in all the talks or choose which ones he/she will give. Also add any notes that will remind you of a personal example you wish to share—or you may write out your examples completely on a separate piece of paper.

The outlines were written with the team in mind so that you would have as little need for advance preparation as possible. However, you should *read the outline out loud several times before presenting it, just to make sure you are comfortable with it and it makes sense to you.* It will also help you to time yourself so that you won't go overtime with too many examples or with sharing that takes too long. The other members of the team should be able to help you with this.

It is important to watch the clock throughout the day and not go overtime. If you promised the couples that they would be finished by 6:00 P.M., be sure to get them out on time. Also, be sure each session starts on time. A few minutes can be made up at lunchtime if necessary.

Sometimes it becomes apparent during a workshop that a point was not clear or at least some of the couples did not understand it. Then you may either handle the questions individually and privately with a couple or you can summarize the point in question for the whole group at the beginning of the next talk. (For example: Begin the next talk by saying, "The question has come up about this statement in our last talk. . ." Then explain the statement.) Often the member of the clergy who is on the team is the most experienced at handling this type of situation and can easily do it.

E. Preparing the Meeting Place for the Workshop

Have an inviting atmosphere. Your own home is an ideal place to have a workshop for the engaged, especially if you have only a few couples. If you have too many couples to comfortably seat in your home or you prefer to work outside your home, choose the most comfortable room available to you. The room should be small enough to feel welcoming, but big enough to allow the couples to spread out a little bit to share with one another. Since the exercises are mixed in with the teaching sections of the talks, it's probably not a good idea to send the couples to separate rooms to share unless you are certain you can get them back within the appropriate time. *If you send them out of the conference room, ask them to write first, before they leave, and give them a definite time when you want them back. Tell them, however, that they can take as long as they need to finish a serious discussion.* You will proceed with the talk.

Someone should check out the facility ahead of time. Leave directions for setting up the meeting room and the break-out rooms. You should be sure there is an adequate number of chairs and tables for lunch. Find out where the restrooms are, how to get into the kitchen, where the coffee pots are kept, how to store cold items, and how to turn on the heat or air conditioning. It's also helpful to know where to park cars, particularly if there will be a church service that day.

A lectern or podium is very helpful for the team if one is available, since *the team will be standing to present their talks.* If presenting to a very large group, you may need a microphone. Two microphones are better than one. You will also need a small table for your notes and other supplies.

F. Presenting the Workshop

[NOTE: The directions below refer to presenting the workshop as a one-day program. However, please note that DAY-BY-DAY *has also been offered as a series of evening sessions. Each of the four evening sessions is approximately two hours long.]*

Plan to have someone *arrive an hour before the program begins* to set up the coffee, arrange the chairs, and handle registration.

Set up a group of chairs, auditorium style, facing the speakers. If there is room, set up more chairs around the room for private sharing, or place tables in the back of the room which can be used for relaxing between talks and for lunch. Make sure there is a lectern or table where the team members can place their notes while speaking. Put the coffee and refreshment table out where it is readily available throughout the day. Make sure you have an adequate number of copies of the printed materials, pens, a Bible, etc.

Before the engaged couples arrive, the team should gather to pray. Invite God to be the center of your time together and to bless your words as you speak them and to bless the participants that they may have "...ears to hear and eyes that see...."

The team should *greet the engaged couples as they come in,* making sure they are registered and have their name-tags. They'll want to know where to find the coffee, put their snacks, and place their coats. Try to make the couples feel as welcome as possible, as you would with guests in your own home.

Plan to offer some refreshments before you begin. Most engaged couples live very busy lives. Some will arrive without having eaten. Some will be exhausted. Some will not have seen one another before the workshop. Some may have been arguing.

Simply having a hot cup of coffee/tea to drink, a cold soft drink, a cookie or doughnut, can help them relax, leave their distractions behind them and get ready to enter into the spirit of the presentations.

To give them time to unwind before you begin, *it's helpful to advertise the day as beginning a half hour before the first session.*

All team members should plan to remain throughout the day. The engaged couples will get the message that the team really cares about them when they see you present all day long. It also helps to convey the message that the faith community really cares about them and is interested in their relationship.

Start the first talk on time. Ask the couples to respect the schedule and to be prompt in reassembling throughout the day.

Those who are presenting the talk will use the lectern or table for their notes. The rest of the team members can sit with the engaged. *When the outline calls for the engaged couples to write, it is recommended that each team couple write and share with their spouse. That makes it a day of enrichment for the whole team.*

The outline contains a recommended time for writing and sharing. Consider this as a minimum, but scan the group and adjust the time accordingly. If the eyes of a majority are looking up during the time for writing, call an end to the time allowed and tell them to go on to their sharing. Likewise, observe them during the sharing time. As a rule when the noise level picks up, it's a sign that the sharing has finished and they're just chatting. If that's the case, it's time to move on.

Normally there is no need for a formal break time between sessions, since the couples drift back into the room and help themselves to refreshments, restrooms, etc.

If some couples planned to go out for a quick lunch, ask them to be back for the next session and give them the estimated starting time for that session.

If you observe a couple having difficulty with the questions or not follow-ing the directions, gently ask them if you can help them. Don't make negative judgments about the couples. You'll be pleasantly surprised at how diligently most will do everything asked of them. Be alert for people who can't read. If you think there is someone, make a general announcement that those having difficulty with the exercises can ask their partners to help them during the sharing time.

At the end of the workshop you might wish to announce that *the engaged couples are invited to keep in touch with the team and their pastor.* If they are experiencing any difficulties in their relationship after marriage, they shouldn't wait until they are deeply troubled. They can contact either the team members or their clergy for assistance.

If you wish, you may *provide the engaged with a list with the team's names, addresses, phone numbers, and church affiliation.*

Relax. With God's help you'll do a great job!

3. Summary

As you begin your ministry as a marriage preparation team, it's impor-tant to remember that *God is not asking you to change the couples you will meet or make them conform to some standard you have in mind for them.* God is only asking you to love them. That you can do—beautifully and simply. The best way to begin is within your own marriage by loving each other.

We keep you in our prayers.

[Sample letter to be sent to confirm registration for engaged couples for the DAY-BY-DAY marriage preparation workshop]

[Date]

Dear (name of participant),

   We look forward to meeting you and spending some time together as you invest this day in preparing for your marriage.

   The purpose of the workshop is to give you a few hours' time away from all the busy-ness of your lives and help you discover even more fully the richness of your love for each other and the love of God for each of you. The workshop will help you communicate more deeply with one another on a variety of issues.

   The DAY-BY-DAY workshop will take place:
   DATE:
   PLACE: (name of building, address, emergency phone number, and directions to the address if necessary)
   TIME: 8:30 A.M.–6:00 P.M.

   There will be coffee and refreshments available when you arrive. Lunch will be provided. Please dress comfortably and bring your favorite snack to share.

   The contribution for the workshop is (*insert correct amount*) and should be paid at sign-in on Saturday morning. Checks may be written to (*name of sponsor of workshop*). If you cannot afford this amount, please let a team member know when you arrive, and suitable arrangements will be made.

   If you have any questions, call (*insert local phone number of contact person*).

In Christ's love,

(signed by contact person)

DAY-BY-DAY
Schedule

SIGN-IN, COFFEE, ETC.	8:30 A.M.–9:00 A.M.
SESSION 1 *Introduction*	9:00 A.M.–10:45 A.M.
SESSION 2 *Communications*	10:45 A.M.–12:15 P.M.
LUNCH	12:15 P.M.–1:15 P.M.
SESSION 3 *Gift of Sexuality*	1:15 P.M.–3:15 P.M.
SESSION 4 *Covenant*	3:15 P.M.–4:45 P.M.
SESSION 5 *Going Forth*	4:45 P.M.–5:00 P.M.
OPTIONAL DINNER	5:00 P.M.–6:00 P.M.

Special Considerations for Second-Time Marriages

Couples entering marriage for the second time are usually more mature (at least in years) than first-time couples and have the advantage of some years of experience in marriage. In fact, many come to marriage preparation classes with resentment since they already know how to budget their money (and may own their own home). They understand sexual intimacy and may already have children. They may ask, *"What more do we need to know?"*

Our response is usually along these lines: "As a faith community, we are obliged to provide you with the best preparation possible for marriage. We want your marriage not only to work, but to be a wonderful experience for you and for us. *Even though you have been married before, you have not been married to each other before.* This is a brand-new relationship with a very different person. Take the time you need to explore this relationship more deeply." People are generally willing to at least give marriage preparation a try.

As a pastor or marriage preparation team, it's important to remember that *the divorce rate for second-time marriages is significantly higher* than for first-time marriages. Depending on which statistics you use, the divorce rate for first-time marriages is 47-50%, and 55-67% for second-time marriages. For couples who enter the second marriage with children under the age of eighteen, the statistics are even worse.

While second-timers have some things working for them, they also bring with them extra challenges and perhaps bad memories from their previous relationships. Their partner, who may never have been married before, may have also had a share of negative relationships. Either one or both parties may also have a strong attachment to their family-of-origin, since their families may have been their sole source of emotional support over the years.

In addition to the regular marriage preparation program offered in DAY-BY-DAY, some of the issues that should be discussed with couples entering second-time marriages are:

1. *Priorities.* The first priority in marriage is the husband/wife relationship. The second priority is immediate family, especially dependent children. For most single parents, their first priority has been their child/children

and many have an uncommon bond of attachment. Some questions the engaged couple need to consider are: *Can* I make you my first priority? *Will* I make you my first priority? On the other hand, will you be flexible enough to allow me to continue to love and nurture my children? Can you share me with them? Will I help them open up and share our world with you? They should also discuss discipline of the children. Will the custodial parent trust the step-parent to care for and discipline the children? (If there is a local step-parenting support group, have that reference available to couples even before they need it.)

2. *Moving.* For couples who share custody of their children with their former spouse, moving out of town can pose a big problem. For others, who have been single for some time, leaving an aging parent/relative may be very difficult. Some questions to discuss now are: If the situation should arise where we have to move out of town or out of state, will you go with me? How will child visitation rights or our relationship with our extended family be affected? If the answer of one of us is, "No, I can't leave town," is that an answer acceptable to both of us?

3. *Future Children.* Some people entering second-time marriages already consider their family complete. They may have one or more children from a previous marriage and not wish to have any more. For the partner who has no children, however, or for the partner who may be a non-custodial parent, the idea of more children can be very appealing. It's a question too few couples seriously consider, but must be dealt with seriously. (In the Catholic Church, the refusal to have children can be an impediment to marriage and should be discussed with a priest before marriage.) Some questions for the couple to discuss are: Am I willing to consider having children with you, or do I consider that phase of my life over? Am I willing to have more children to please you?

4. *Finances.* Some come into second-time marriages with considerable financial assets. If they have children from a previous marriage, financial arrangements should be made ahead of time about how they will handle gifts, education, and inheritance rights for your children/my children/our children. Some people give up alimony and other benefits from their first marriage when they remarry. In that case, it needs to be made clear how they will be provided for if something happens to their new spouse. Professional financial counseling may be a good idea for some couples *before* they marry.

5. *Child Support.* Some parents have extensive child support or alimony payments due each month to a previous spouse. Without heroic effort on the partner's part, these can be a source of continual strife in the new marriage. Yet to support all children conceived inside or outside of marriage is essential and is a normal Christian responsibility. Some questions to con-

sider: Am I willing to encourage you to continue your efforts to support your child/children both financially and emotionally? Am I willing to continue working if necessary to help make it possible for you to maintain a level of support to them? If we have children of our own and we both have to continue working in order for you to support your child/children, how will I feel?

6. *Ex-Spouse.* When there are children involved, the first spouse is almost always an on-going part of life in the second marriage. Some questions to discuss are: How does your/my relationship with a previous spouse affect our relationship now? How will this change after we are married?

The DAY-BY-DAY book can be very helpful for follow-up discussions with couples entering second-time marriages. *Three exercises that will be particularly helpful to them are:*

1. When You're Having an Argument.
2. When the Hurt Lingers On.
3. When You Are Disappointed in One Another.

Point out these exercises and go over them with the couples before the wedding if possible. Very often they did not handle conflict well in their first marriage and they may also be carrying emotional baggage from their previous relationship(s). Sometimes, if the new marriage partner inadvertently says or does something to remind the other of the previous partner, it is easy to fly off the handle and take offense, when no offense is intended. In that case, such persons need to forgive either their ex-spouse or themselves for mistakes made in the past. Some may also need to let go of any grudges against God, particularly if they believe God was not there for them or did not answer their prayers.

It is not uncommon for a person who was married to an alcoholic the first time to choose to marry a recovering alcoholic in the second marriage. If this is the case, we advise them to continue to be involved in Al-Anon and AA. These groups will keep them honest about the use/abuse of drugs and alcohol and help prevent a recurrence of previous unhealthy behavior.

Below you'll find a summary of the questions couples entering second-time marriages should discuss before marrying.

Some Questions To Consider

The following questions should be discussed before you get married. In this way, you'll know fully what to expect from one another as you enter your marriage. Many of the questions may not apply to you, especially if your children are grown or you have no children. In that case, you may need to consider your relationship with any person who is close to you and has depended on you, such as an aging parent.

1. *Can* I make you my first priority?

2. *Will* I make you my first priority?

3. Will you be flexible enough to allow me to continue to love and nurture my children? Can you share me with them?

4. Will I help my family open up and share our world with you?

5. Do I trust you enough to allow you to discipline my children? What rules about behavior do we both want to have in our home? Do I think you are or will be a good mother/good father?

6. If the situation should arise where we have to move out-of-town or out-of-state, will you go with me? How will child visitation rights or our relationship with our extended family be affected? If the answer of one of us is, "No, I can't leave town," is that an answer acceptable to both of us?

7. Am I willing to consider having children with you—or do I consider that phase of my life over? Am I willing to have more children to please you?

8. Have we discussed and do we agree about financial arrangements such as gifts, education and inheritance rights for your children/my children/our children? Have we discussed how either of us will be provided for if something should happen to one of us? Have we settled what we'll do with any financial assets with which we enter marriage? Am I willing to see a professional financial counselor to help us if necessary?

9. Am I willing to encourage you to continue your efforts to support your child/children both financially and emotionally? Am I willing to continue working if necessary to help make it possible for you to maintain a level of support to them?

10. If we have children of our own and we both continue working in order for you to support your child/children, how will I feel?

11. How does your/my relationship with a previous spouse affect our relationship now? How do your/my memories of that relationship affect us? How will this change?

Session One Introduction and Expectations (Scripture: 1 Cor 13:1-13)

[Before each talk, set up the appropriate scripture verses in the Bible so you won't have to fumble through the pages later on.]

I. On behalf of the whole team, I offer a warm welcome to all of you.

II. You have come to the church to ask the Lord's blessing on your marriage.

A. You have indicated by this gesture that God is important to you. You want God to be a part of your lives together and your love for one another.

B. As we begin, we're going to pray together that God will be with us (the team) and you as we prepare together for your marriage.

C. *Prayer*

[NOTE: One member of the team prays for the grace of openness to the Holy Spirit, that God will send us the Spirit to guide us in all we do today and bless our efforts as we work to deepen our love relationships. Mention any distractions the couples may have come in with or concerns you believe may be present. Your pastor may be able to help you with this. Typical examples of distractions may be:

1. Fear of what we'll learn about each other.
2. Fear that we won't be allowed to have a church wedding if we don't "pass the course."
3. Fear that my partner won't marry me if I'm completely honest with him/her.

4. I'm too tired to get anything out of this.
5. I resist this because I already know everything I need to know.
6. I don't have time for all this. I have many other things to do.

As you pray, mention any barriers or distractions that come to mind. Ask God to lift them from us.

[After the Prayer: Take a few minutes to explain the facilities—where the restrooms are located, and where coffee and other beverages and refreshments are available all day, to which they are invited to help themselves whenever they wish. Tell them the schedule for the day and that all talks will start on time.]

III. Introductions

A. Good morning. It is good to be with you for our Christian marriage preparation program. We call it DAY-BY-DAY, because our marriages are a lifelong daily process of growing in love, not just a one-time ceremony that publicly announces our commitment to each other and sends us on our way.

B. This day is meant just for the two of you. It's an opportunity to come together without all the distractions of daily life, such as jobs, friends, in-laws, wedding preparations, and, for some, care of your children, etc.

C. Although there are many other wonderful people here today, we encourage you to spend your time here together as a couple—to focus on one another, and really listen to everything your fiancée has to say.

D. We are _____.
   We are from (*name of church*).
   We have been married for ___ years and are the parents of _____ (*number of children*).

E. [NOTE: The rest of the team introduce themselves in the same way.]

F. Now we will go around the room and invite each of you to share with us your name, the name of the church in which your wedding will be held, and your wedding date.

[NOTE: Allow time for introductions. The couples can either sit or stand when they speak.]

IV. Why are we here?

A. You are probably wondering why your pastor asked you to come here for the DAY-BY-DAY workshop. Why are you asked to add one more task to an already stressful time for you as you prepare for your wedding?

B. We are here because we care about you and we care about your marriage. We want you to have the best possible start on your Christian marriage.

C. You may notice that the team will be reading the talks. This is to ensure that all the points are made within the time allowed. It is also because we are not professionals. We were chosen by our pastors to be here with you, and to share our experiences of Christian marriage. We'll be honest with our personal sharing and ask you to do the same with each other.

D. It's our hope that your participation in DAY-BY-DAY will add to the depth of love you already have for one another. As you learn more about each other and come to understand each other more fully, you thank God who has brought such a wonderful person into your life. God did this so you can more clearly know how special you are and how much God loves you.

E. Most likely your parents and grandparents did not go to a marriage preparation program. But today we expect more from marriage, and we can expect to live together in Christian marriage far longer than our ancestors did.

1. If you had gotten married in the 1800s, the twenty-five year-long marriage was considered a great accomplishment. Most people died early, and women often died at childbirth.

   (a) The average couple who got married in 1860 would spend only a few years together without children in the course of their entire marriage.
   (b) The roles played by men and women were firmly established. Their lives centered on earning a living and raising a family. If they fulfilled those roles they were considered to have a successful marriage.

2. The average couple married in the 1960s could look forward to reaching their fiftieth anniversary, of which approximately twenty years would be spent without children in their home.

   (a) These couples married with the same role-oriented expectations that their parents had: marriage was about parenting and providing.
   (b) But times have changed dramatically in the last thirty years; so have our expectations for a good marriage. If our parents have failed to develop their relationship, or to increase their communication skills, and not really worked at understanding each other, they may find

themselves deeply troubled in their marriages even though they have been both good parents and good providers.

(c) Today the divorce rate for marriages over twenty years is rapidly growing. It is a concern to all of us, and one of the major reasons that the churches offer preparation programs like this one.

3. Because of increased life-expectancy and improved health care, the average couple marrying today can expect to spend fifty to sixty years in their marriage relationship.

(a) You will probably have an average of thirty years together in which you are not raising your children.

(b) You will probably expect a great deal more of one another than your grandparents did, and you will renegotiate your marriage relationship five to ten times during your married life. If you ignore the need for on-going change and growth, you risk divorce, or a lonely life together.*

F. When we marry, we're most likely looking for someone with whom we can talk, work, play, and pray—someone who will understand us in all the peak moments and stand at our side through all the dark moments of our life.

G. This is why we gather today.

1. Throughout the day, we'll have a series of short presentations by the team, to get you thinking about the topics.

2. Then we'll ask you to write down your own attitudes about the topic. We will give you check-lists to help you do this. There are no right or wrong answers—there are only *your* answers, and they describe your opinion today.

3. This is not a test. The team will not see your answers. You will keep everything you write and take it home with you. No one will see your notes except your future spouse.

H. Now we'll give each of you a copy of the first exercise and ask you to reflect for a few moments about why you are here today. Write your responses to the questions in Exercise 1.1.

[NOTE: In order to model for the couples what kind of responses we expect them to make, before they begin to write one team member reads each question aloud and shares his/her answer.]

Then encourage them to be honest with one another. These answers are for their eyes only. They will not be asked to share any of their answers today with anyone other than their partner. Allow 5 minutes for their writing and

[NOTE: For more information, refer to Liturgy Training Publications, 155 E. Superior St., Chicago, IL 60611.]

then ask them to remain in their places and quietly share their responses with each other. Allow 5–10 minutes for their sharing.

Exercise 1.1

Put a check mark next to all answers which apply to you. There is a space at the end (Other_____) to write in your own reason if none of the rest apply to you.

A. Why did I come here today?
__ I love you very much.
__ I'm willing to go anywhere for you.
__ I felt forced to come.
__ I came to learn more about you.
__ Our pastor told us to come.
__ I wanted to please you.
__ I want to give our marriage the best possible start.
__ Some friends have come and liked it.
__ I'm not sure why I came.
__ Other _____

B. What do I hope to gain here today?
__ Deeper awareness of you.
__ Increasing love for you.
__ To learn more about what a Christian marriage is.
__ Peace of mind.
__ Insight into myself.
__ The skills I need for a great marriage.
__ A few hours to talk with you without distractions.
__ Answers to some of my questions.
__ I honestly don't expect to gain anything.
__ Other _____

[After you finish writing, exchange your answer sheets and share your answers with your fiancé. You can stay right where you are seated and talk softly to each other. Be sure to tell one another *why* you answered as you did. You'll have about 5 minutes to do this.]

[NOTE: *Allow the couples 5–10 minutes for sharing. Then ask for their attention as one team member reads aloud directly from the Bible. All scripture readings are from* New Oxford Annotated Bible, *edited by Bruce Metzger and Roland E. Murphy, Oxford University Press, New York, 1991.*]

V. Scripture Reading   1 Cor 13:1-13

If I speak in the tongues of mortals and of angels but do not have love, I am a noisy gong or a clanging cymbal. And if I have prophetic powers, and understand all mysteries and all knowledge, and if I have all faith, so as to remove mountains, but do not have love, I am nothing. If I give away all my possessions, and if I hand over my body so that I may boast, but do not have love, I gain nothing.

Love is patient; love is kind; love is not envious or boastful or arrogant or rude. It does not rejoice in wrong-doing, but rejoices in the truth. It bears all things, believes all things, hopes all things, endures all things.

Love never ends. But as for prophecies, they will come to an end; as for tongues, they will cease; as for knowledge, it will come to an end. For we know only in part, and we prophesy only in part; but when the complete comes, the partial will come to an end. When I was a child, I spoke like a child, I thought like a child, I reasoned like a child; when I became an adult, I put an end to childish ways. For now we see in a mirror dimly, but then we will see face to face. Now I know only in part; then I will know fully; even as I have been fully known. And now faith, hope, and love abide, these three; and the greatest of these is love.

A. This beautiful passage from scripture affirms who we are and how we are to live—as lovers of God and one another.

B. If we have love and live in love, we have the greatest of all the spiritual gifts.

C. But living in love is not always easy—even when we are trying. In the course of every marriage we find that just as we can be each other's greatest blessing, we can also be each other's greatest cross.

D. As you look around today at all the married couples you know (parents, grandparents, brothers/sisters, cousins, friends, those with whom you work, etc.), how many are living in what you would call joyful, happy marriages? How many have settled for just getting along, or are really struggling to survive?

E. How many of the marriages you see on TV or in the movies are really great Christian marriages? How many are based on put-downs, manipulation, unkindness, pride, arrogance, or greed—all those things that St. Paul reminds us fail to make love grow.

F. What kind of marriage do you want? *You are free to choose.* Most of us have no control over the political issues of our day, the security of our jobs or investments, or what the future holds in store for us.

G. The one thing we can control is the quality of our love for one another. When all else fails, we still have one another if we are willing to work on our marriage DAY-BY-DAY.

1. In our society there is some concern about whether two people can actually stay in love.

   (a) We hear talk of "falling in love," as though we were helpless to control ourselves, like catching a cold or the flu.
   (b) Then we fear it must be possible to "fall out of love." We fear that someday we too might "lose those lovin' feelings."

2. But love is more than just a feeling. Love includes the good feelings like caring, warmth, affection, desire, joy in one another and so much more.

3. But essentially, *love is a decision*. At some point in your courtship you have decided to love one another. You have taken an honest look at one another, and decided, "Yes, you are the one. I can love you forever." You can even list all the reasons why this person is just the right person for you.

4. Love is a decision throughout our lives. Even when we don't *feel* particularly loving, we can *decide* to act in love with one another. Even when we don't want to practice those qualities listed by St. Paul, we can decide to do so.

5. We are in control of love in our relationship! We can freely decide to live in love twenty-four hours a day, every day of our lives. That's how God loves us.

H. What do you expect from your marriage and your life together? It's important to get in touch with our hopes and dreams in order to understand what we both want in our relationship.

I. Now we'll give you Exercise 1.2. Then I will share what my hopes and dreams were for our marriage before we got married. I'll also tell you how I would like to be able to describe my marriage to my grandchildren when I'm seventy years old.

   [NOTE: One team member shares responses to questions. Then give the couples 5–10 minutes for writing their responses. Then call time and ask them to share their responses with each other for 5–10 minutes. If you are using other rooms for the couples' sharing, send them there after they have written. Follow this pattern for each exercise.]

Exercise 1.2

A. What would you like your life/your marriage to be like one year from now? (Where will you be living? Will you have children? How will you behave toward one another?)

_____

_____

B. What would you like your life/your marriage to be like ten years from now? (Where will you be living? Will you have children? How will you behave toward one another?)

_____

_____

C. What beautiful qualities of love as mentioned in St. Paul's letter do you see in your beloved? Describe the evidence.

__	Patience	__	Kindness
__	Inner peace	__	Humility
__	Generosity of spirit	__	Tactful
__	Giving	__	Inner joy
__	Forgiving	__	Understanding
__	Compassion	__	Persevering
__	Faithfulness	__	Rejoices in the truth
__	Love of God	__	Deeply caring
__	Other (_____)		

[Put a check mark next to the strongest quality. When do you see that most fully present in your beloved?]

_____

_____

_____

D. When you are seventy years old, how would you like to be able to describe your life and marriage to your grandchildren? What would you have hoped your life together would have been like?

_____

_____

_____

When you finish writing, exchange what you have written and compare your answers with each other. How do you agree? How do you disagree?

[NOTE: Allow 5–10 minutes for writing responses, and another 10 minutes for the couples to share with each other. Tell them when to return to the conference room.]

Session Two
Getting To Know You—
Communications
(Scripture: John 17:11-13)

[NOTE: Throughout this talk the team may add their own experiences to highlight the points being made. Always use brief examples. We want to allow the couples their full amount of time for sharing in each exercise.]

I. Good communications are the rock on which every strong relationship builds. They are fundamental and essential to a good marriage.

A. To communicate deeply and honestly with another person and to be understood and accepted by the other draws the two people into deep intimacy—the intimacy on which a healthy sexual relationship develops and in which the problems of life can be faced in trust and openness.

B. Communicating with our beloved also teaches us about ourselves as we explore attitudes, opinions, and feelings about who I am, and who you are, and who we are in the world.

C. Communication is the act of becoming one. Jesus' prayer for his disciples at the last supper was that they would be one. These are his words:

[NOTE: Read aloud the verses below. Read directly from a Bible. That is a visual sign to the couples that these words are from scripture.]

Holy Father, protect them in your name that you have given me, so that they may be one. While I was with them, I protected them in your name that you have given me. I guarded them, and not one of them was lost except the one destined to be lost, so that the scripture might be fulfilled. But now I am coming to you, and I speak these things in the world so that they may have my joy made complete in themselves.   (Jn 17:11-13)

1. As Christians, we are called to be one. Nowhere is that call so demanding or so urgent as in marriage, for in our oneness we will know complete joy—the joy that Jesus wants for us.

2. In this day of sexual liberation, many couples have no difficulty in starting a sexual relationship. Some believe that if they have good sex, everything else will take care of itself. But that's not true.

3. Once a couple has sex before marriage, they often don't establish lines of verbal communication between them, or do so only on a surface level.

4. Becoming one as husband and wife certainly includes a sexual relationship, but it also includes emotional and spiritual intimacy as well. This can only be done through on-going verbal and non-verbal communication.

5. Sometimes it is more difficult to be emotionally naked in front of the one we love than it is to be physically naked.

II. The root meaning of the word "intimacy" is "with fear."

A. Most couples want intimacy with one another but are afraid of it.

B. Much depends on the way you were raised, what your experiences have been like in previous relationships, and on your self-confidence and your confidence in your partner.

C. Sharing yourself deeply with another person and trusting the other person to be open to receiving you always involves an element of risk.

D. It takes a great deal of trust to become truly intimate.

E. Let's look at a list of reasons why some people find it difficult to communicate.

[NOTE: Hand out Exercise 2.1. Go through the directions briefly. One member of the team briefly shares his/her responses to the questions today. Tell the couples they can go to another place for sharing and return to the conference room in 20 minutes. Allow about 20 minutes for the exercise and then resume the presentation.]

Exercise 2.1

A. Below are listed a number of reasons why some people find it difficult to communicate or to talk honestly about their deepest feelings. Go through the list and put a check mark next to every reason why you may find it difficult to share with your partner on at least some areas of your relationship.

ME	MY PARTNER	
___	___	I don't know how.
___	___	I didn't know I'd be asked to do this.
___	___	I'm afraid to make you angry.
___	___	I'm not sure I want to get into this.
___	___	I have been hurt before by *someone else*. I'm afraid to trust again.
___	___	I've been hurt before by *you*. I'm afraid to trust again.
___	___	We never have much time to talk without distractions.
___	___	My family never did this.
___	___	None of our friends does this and they seem to be doing all right.
___	___	I don't see myself as a very "deep" person.
___	___	If I tell you everything about me, will you still want to marry me?
___	___	We're usually too tired to talk.
___	___	I don't want to start a fight.
___	___	I'm hoping you'll change after we're married.
___	___	I'm afraid of a broken engagement or postponed wedding.
___	___	I worry about whether we'll be able to work through our differences if we open up a difficult issue.
___	___	Other_____

Now go back through the list and put a check mark next to every reason why you believe your fiancé may hold back in sharing with you, at least in some areas.

Identify an area where you would like to know your fiancé's feelings more clearly.

_____

Identify an area where you would like to explain your feelings more clearly to your fiancé.

_____

B. Below are some stereotypical statements often made about men and women that may or may not be true for the two of you. Go through the list and put a check mark next to each statement you believe is true for you.

Men write in the HIS column; women write in the HERS column. Then go back through the list and put a * next to each statement you believe describes your fiancé.

HIS	HERS	
—	—	Men are directed outward.
—	—	Women are directed inward.
—	—	A man's self-image focuses on "what I do."
—	—	A woman's self-image focuses on "who I am."
—	—	Men tend to be competitive.
—	—	Women tend to value cooperation.
—	—	Men value independence.
—	—	Women value interdependence.
—	—	Women talking to women stress their feelings and emphasize relationships.
—	—	Men talking to men stress external events, what they accomplished, happenings in the world of sports, etc.
—	—	Men don't pay much attention to feelings.
—	—	Women pay a lot of attention to sharing of feelings.
—	—	Men tend to be goal-oriented. "We made that decision. Let's move on to something else."
—	—	Women tend to be process-oriented. "I've changed my mind. I want to discuss that decision again."
—	—	Women are more likely to press for good communications than men.

Take a few minutes to share your answers with one another.

[NOTE: Allow 15 minutes for the couples to do the exercise and then resume the presentation.]

Wrap Up

It's often true that women are more likely to press for good verbal communications than men.

Some men enjoy what they can see and experience in their wives: her body, the way she keeps house, the way she loves him and makes love to him, the way she cares for their children, her success in her career, etc.

Most women want their husbands to know and love what cannot be seen: her heart and soul. She wants to love her husband in the same way. She really does want to know what's going on inside of him. Often her husband doesn't know how to put his feelings into words to describe them to her or even to himself.

A man might say, "I talked at work all day. I don't want to talk anymore when I get home. What do we have to talk about anyway? We've already said it all."

A wife might respond, "I need to know the real you, and I need to reveal to you the real me." She believes that what makes her special is not her outer beauty which will eventually fade, but her inner beauty which will grow with time.

Both men and women fear losing themselves and their self-identity by becoming one with the other. The paradox is that we get a clearer picture of who we are as individuals and as a couple when we live in deep intimacy.

III. Prayer

[NOTE: Invite the couples to hold hands with one another as one person on the team leads the prayer and they follow in the silence of their hearts.]

Pray for *The Grace of Trust and Confidence in My Fiancé—For Openness in Communicating Between the Two of Us.*

[NOTE: Mention any fears you believe may be present in yourself or the group. You may refer back to any of the concerns mentioned in Exercise 2.1, or any you sense in the participants, such as fear of being out of control, fear of saying something to hurt you, etc.]

Ask God to lift our fears from us and free us to be as open and honest as we can possibly be with one another so that our love can grow more deeply than ever before.

IV. Most couples don't try to keep secrets from one another. Often the reason why people may not discuss a topic before they are married is simply because the issue never came up or because they assumed there was no need for discussion.

A. Often the issues that are never discussed become the issues that are most divisive after marriage—topics like the division of household chores, attitudes about money, and care and discipline of the children. These are the molehills that become mountains.

B. Therefore it's helpful to get as many issues as possible out in the open before marriage to make sure we have a clear understanding about what's expected after marriage.

C. Once in a while, some couples will refuse to face up to an issue before marriage because they fear a broken engagement or do not want to postpone their wedding.

  1. Issues don't go away by ignoring them. It's essential that you face up to your differences as well as your similarities.
  2. Sometimes issues seem bigger than they really are when they're not

39

discussed. By discussing something that seems like a major problem to one of us, we may find that it's not a problem to our fiancé at all. We may have made a mountain out of a molehill.

D. Sometimes we believe we're keeping a carefully hidden secret from our fiancé and we're afraid to reveal it. Often we may be surprised that our fiancé guessed our secret some time ago and still loves us.

E. We urge you today to be open and honest with one another—to place your love and trust in your fiancé.

1. You should share anything about yourself that will affect your life together in the future: financial debts, previous marriages or children (not the details but the fact that they exist), health, drug/alcohol use, tendency toward physical violence, ability or desire to have children, or a previous love affair that isn't quite over.

2. You need not share any information that will be detrimental to your relationship—especially the details of past romantic involvements that are truly over.

V. Since we tend to adopt the communications style of our family-of-origin and bring it into our own marriage, it's helpful to understand our underlying attitudes about how communications should be handled. Let's go to Exercise 2.2.

[NOTE: Hand out Exercise 2.2—one copy for each participant. Go over the directions and briefly summarize how one member of the team answered the questions.]

Exercise 2.2

A. Below are a series of statements about your family-of-origin and how they communicated with one another. On the left hand side, under the column *MY FAMILY*, check all those statements that apply to your family-of-origin. If you grew up in more than one home, or were adopted, choose the answers which applied most of the time. On the right hand side, under the column *OUR MARRIAGE*, put a check mark after each statement you want to put into practice *in your own home*.

MY
FAMILY   OUR
MARRIAGE

___   We never lied to one another.   ___
___   We were always able to express feelings honestly.   ___
___   We were never too tired or too preoccupied to listen.

___ We often only partially listened to each other. ___

___ We didn't make snap judgments about the other person. ___

___ We often spoke before the other finished talking. ___

___ We often shouted, pounded a fist, or waved our arms to make a point. ___

___ We always faced up to our differences. ___

___ We complimented one another often. ___

___ We always looked for the goodness in one another. ___

___ Criticism was a regular part of life. ___

___ We called each other names. ___

___ We did much good-natured teasing. ___

___ We laughed a great deal and had fun together. ___

___ One member of the family was always tense or defensive. ___

___ We thought shouting helped us make our point. ___

___ Slamming a door or leaving the house was often part of an argument. ___

___ Some family members stopped speaking to each other rather than argue. ___

___ Not speaking to each other is a regular form of punishment in my family. ___

___ We turned off TV/radio or put down a newspaper to pay attention to each other. ___

___ We made time to be together just to enjoy one another's company. ___

___ My parents kept secrets from each other. ___

___ Only weak people cried in front of each other. ___

___ We were openly affectionate with one another. ___

___ My parents often had intimate talks together. ___

___ Forgiveness was a normal part of making up. ___

___ There were no "winners" or "losers" in an argument. ___

___ When angry, it was permissible to sulk and/or pout. ___

___ Sulking and pouting helped me get my way. ___

___ Swearing was common in our house. ___

___ We had many secrets from each other. ___

___ Telling the truth was important. ___

___ In an argument people sometimes hit each other. ___

___ I sometimes hit people when I'm angry. ___

___ Mom and dad often spoke the words "I love you" to me and others. ___

___ My parents were openly affectionate with each other. ___

___ Arguing was not permitted in my family. ___

___ It's easier to show my love than to speak it directly. ___

___ I find it difficult to confront issues directly. ___

___ When you ask me what's wrong, I deny anything is wrong. ___

___ The men in our family refuse to communicate. ___

___ Women in our family manipulate others to get their way. ___

B. Of all the items listed above, which do you regard as the strongest points (best qualities) in your relationship right now? (Put a * next to your strong points.)

C. Of all the items listen above, which do you regard as the weakest points in your relationship right now? (Put an X next to the weak points of either you or your future spouse.)

D. What did your family do that you would least like to see repeated in your own marriage?

_____

_____

E. What did your family do that you would most like to see repeated in your own marriage?

_____

_____

F. What change can you make right now in order to communicate better with your partner?

_____

_____

G. What change would you like your partner to make in order to help you communicate better as a couple?

_____

_____

H. I believe we should communicate deeply with each other _____ _____ (How frequently?)

I. The best time for us to communicate is

_____

_____

As soon as your partner is done, share your answers with each other and discuss them in some detail. Take the time you need to fully explain yourself and to truly understand one another.

[NOTE: Team allows 20 minutes for the couples to do the exercise. Tell the couples to come back in 20 minutes. Then resume the presentation.]

Wrap Up

By understanding the emotional style of each of our families-of-origin, we understand more what we can expect of one another in marriage.

If your partner came from a family where all emotions were suppressed and anger was never allowed, then the first time you explode in anger, your partner will assume, "I've married a madman/madwoman."

If one of you came from a family that offered the cold, silent treatment for days on end, the other might come to believe, "He/she doesn't even love me enough to fight with me." Abuse and violence are *never* acceptable in a marriage relationship. If you are in a relationship where violence (or the threat of violence) is used, postpone your wedding until after you've successfully concluded counseling.

It's essential to face up to the issues that arise between us in marriage and not ignore them and spend days together in silence.

Two people who are living together for a lifetime will certainly have differences of opinion arise at least occasionally, and sometimes quite often.

Having an argument does not mean we have a bad marriage. It simply means there is an issue about which we both feel strongly, and quite possibly we are both right.

Facing up to our differences helps us grow in our understanding of ourselves and one another and to clear the air.

There is a way to fight constructively and you will find some ideas listed in the take-home book chapter entitled "When You Are Having an Argument." Read them (as a couple) thoroughly before your next argument.

VI. Conversation is easier and safer than communication

A. We will have very few intimate relationships. With most people we only need to exchange information, attitudes and opinions.

B. For example, people at the bus stop, the people with whom we work, most of our friends, or those with whom we play ball, or attend parties—with them we only enjoy a surface relationship. We can talk easily about the weather, sports, TV programs, or the latest news.

C. There are some with whom we have a long-standing close relationship—our mom or dad, brother/sister, or a very close friend, etc. So we may reveal more of ourselves to them and have close moments when we're on the same wavelength.

VII. Going Deeper

A. In marriage, communication is not an option. We must communicate with one another (both verbally and non-verbally) in order to have true intimacy, and we must communicate our feelings as well as our thoughts and opinions.

B. Chances are you are already communicating ideas, attitudes, opinions, beliefs.

1. It's easy to do. It's what we do on a date as we get to know one another. We ask questions such as: "What kind of music do you like?" "What's your family like?" "What kind of family life do you want?" We talk about our jobs or our favorite team.
2. Hopefully you agree on most of these things. It's important to have shared goals, values, and dreams.
3. But there is even more to learn and understand about each other—our feelings.

C. A feeling is a pleasurable or painful sensation inside us, which may have been aroused by an exterior event or by something interior.

1. We can agree/disagree with one another indefinitely about our attitudes and ideas and argue each other into the ground.
2. But feelings are much deeper—part of the core of who we are. And our feelings are always changing.
3. They arise spontaneously within us. They may not even be rational. We may not even know where they come from. For example, I may get up in the morning feeling irritable. I say, "I got up on the wrong side of the bed." On another day I might feel joyful. We don't usually know how to explain where these feelings came from.
4. We may also both have the same opinion but have very different feelings about it.

   For example, let's say you and your fiancé both believe: "Every couple should postpone having a family until they have been married at least five years."

   Underneath these opinions, your feelings may be very different. One of you may have a deep longing for a baby now. Your feelings may be yearning, loneliness, hunger, and regret about the decision to wait.

   The other person may feel frightened and anxious about becoming a parent and may feel contentment with the decision.

   You can argue about whether or not it's a wise decision to have a baby, but the feelings remain. You can choose to override them, but you should not ignore them. When a couple indefinitely ignores the deep feelings of either one or both of them, they begin to pull away from each other.

44

It's also true that if we are deeply attentive to what our husband /wife is telling us and absorbing the pain, the loneliness, the discomfort that the other is experiencing, regardless of the issue, we will have to continue to work on the issue and come to some peaceful, mutually agreeable solution.

E. I cannot change my spouse, but I can change myself. My reason for deciding to change is based on how my current behavior causes my fiancé discomfort or pain. In other words, I decide to change because I don't want to see my beloved suffer.

F. Feelings are facts—and must be considered in all decision making.

G. We also can't blame one another for our feelings. The feelings simply are. Perhaps they're part of our dream for what our life would be like or part of our expectation of what our marriage should provide.

H. Sometimes we also project our feelings on each other. Perhaps something our spouse says or does reminds us of something that happened in a past relationship, so we lash out at the spouse.

   1. We need to share our feelings and take responsibility for them.
   2. "It's not your fault I feel this way. Even if you did something that offended me, I am responsible for my reaction." In fact, every time you find yourself over-reacting to a situation, stop and ask yourself, "What is there about *me* that causes me to act this way?"

I. Here is a brief exercise to help you sort out a thought from a feeling. Turn to Exercise 2.3 and complete the simple sentences. There is a list of feeling-words to help you. It will only take a few minutes to briefly share your answers with your partner. Please stay here for this sharing.

Exercise 2.3

Complete the following sentences, using only one word (you might wish to refer to the list of feeling-words below):

How do you feel right now?
I feel_____.

I am _____.

List of feeling-words:

happy, sad, bitter, bored, afraid, eager, nervous, anxious, hurt, sincere, delighted, excited, irritable, angry, joyful, tired.

Describe your feeling. How strong is it? (Use a scale of 1 to 10, where 1 is very weak and 10 is very strong.)

_____.

What are your thoughts about having this feeling right now?

I think _____.

I feel that _____.

Now share your responses with your fiancé for a few minutes.

[NOTE: Allow a few minutes to share and then resume the presentation.]

Wrap Up

Whenever we can substitute the words "I am" for "I feel" and still write a meaningful sentence, we can be assured that we have described a feeling—for example, "I feel happy" and "I am happy." Note how often people use the sentence, "I feel that _____." They are not describing a feeling; it is a judgment, opinion, or idea.

VIII. We need to distinguish between listening and hearing.

A. Hearing focuses on self—on making sure I get accurate information. A tape recorder is a perfect hearer.

B. Listening focuses on the other person. Here are some ways to be a better listener to your partner. Since we're going to ask you to do this in a few minutes, please pay close attention to what we are saying.

1. Look into each other's eyes.
2. Hold hands.
3. Pay attention—no distractions. Put other activities aside. Turn off radio, TV, music, etc.
4. Read non-verbal as well as verbal communication, e.g. tears forming in the eyes, tension in the face, wringing of hands, etc.
5. Give positive feedback. "What I hear you saying is…Is that correct?"
6. Restate the case if necessary.
7. Don't listen with your motor running, waiting your turn so you can say what you have to say.
8. Do not tell the other person not to feel that way.

C. Communicating doesn't need to take a lot of time. Let's do a listening exercise to demonstrate how well two people can communicate in less than 5 minutes.

[NOTE: The following listening exercise is not a written exercise. Two members of the team will read the directions and demonstrate the exercise. Then keep time for the participants while they do the exercise with each other.]

Listening Exercise

1. Choose a topic about which you urgently wish to communicate with your partner—wedding plans, in-laws, a strong belief or opinion you have, etc.

2. One of you will be the listener and one of you will be the speaker. Choose right now which of you will go first. That person is the speaker.

3. The speaker talks for 1 minute to the listener about the topic he/she has chosen, expressing not only beliefs and opinions but feelings as well.

4. The listener listens as intently as possible (holding hands, looking into the speaker's eyes, reading the body language of the speaker, looking for clues bchind all that is being said.)

5. After 1 minute, the team will stop the speaker and the listener will feed back what he/she heard the speaker say. The listener has 1 minute to respond without being interrupted. Report back what you saw and read into the speaker's words by his/her body language as well as by his/her actual words.

6. After 1 minute, the team will stop the listener and give the speaker 30 seconds to respond and correct the listener if necessary.

7. Then we will ask you to switch roles. The speaker will become the listener and the listener will become the speaker and we'll repeat the exercise.

   [NOTE: The team demonstrates the procedure. Then direct the couples to do the exercise. One team member keeps time and shouts it out—60 seconds, 30 seconds, etc.]

IX. When a couple communicates well, they find themselves falling more deeply in love, coming to a deeper understanding of one another and finding more peace between and within themselves.

A. You will find that God has sent you a soul-mate, someone who knows what it's like to be you and who loves you because you are you.

B. You will draw closer to one another and grow in knowledge and understanding of each other. You will learn about the awesome rewards of risking, forgiving and reconciling with each other.

C. You will have a deeper awareness of how much God loves you because you have experienced the love of God in your beloved.

D. Communications is a lifetime process. Because we are always changing, we need never grow bored with one another or tired of marriage to the same person.

   [NOTE: Ask them to put their papers inside their folders. It's time for lunch. You might like to lead the group in a prayer of blessing before the meal. Tell them the starting time for the next session.]

Session Three
The Gift of Sexuality
(Scripture: Genesis 2:18-25,
Song of Solomon 8:6-7)

[NOTE: Throughout this talk the team may add their own experiences to highlight the points being made. Always use brief examples. We want to allow the couples their full amount of time for sharing in each exercise.]

I. Throughout history the gift of sexuality has often been misused and misunderstood.

A. It has often not been seen as a gift at all, but as a burden we must tolerate.

B. In many families sexuality has been treated as something dirty or shameful. The domestic issues of today include abuse and incest. If you have been either a victim or perpetrater of abuse, it can be a painful experience to discuss this with your partner. You may need professional counseling. If you have been abused and have not had counseling, talk to your pastor about getting help.

C. Today many people treat sexuality strictly as an activity—something to do on a date — or as a commodity — a way to sell yourself or to sell something to others. In our culture sexuality is equated with lust or pornography, and it has distorted our understanding of the gift of sexuality.

D. It's difficult to rid ourselves of all the misinformation, suggestive advertising, bad teaching, bad experiences and previous history we share in this area.

E. Psychologists tell us that 90% of our sexual stimulation comes from our brain, so it is essential that we look at how we have been influenced by the society in which we live.

F. As Christians we believe that our sexuality is a gift from God. In order to understand our sexuality most fully, we must view it through the eyes of God. We have to set aside all that is unhealthy in our past and open ourselves to God's wisdom.

II. Prayer

[NOTE: Offer a spontaneous prayer, asking God to open our minds and hearts to listen and understand God's view of sexuality. Mention any barriers we may have to receiving this grace—openness to God's view of sexuality—such as:

- I already know everything I need to know.
- I feel guilty and threatened.
- I'm uncomfortable with the topic.
- I'd rather not talk about it.
- I don't want to change my attitudes or behavior.

Add any personal barriers you may have or any you believe should be mentioned with this particular group of couples. Ask God to lift our barriers so we may receive a full measure of this grace of openness to God's view of sexuality.]

III. Introduction to Exercise 3.1

A. The challenge most married couples face today is usually not lack of knowledge about the basics of sexual intercourse between a man and a woman. However, you might want to talk to your pastor if you have some questions.

B. Most people today have adequate knowledge of what is expected on their wedding night. What we lack are wholesome, healthy attitudes about the relationship between men and women.

C. Our attitudes shape our behavior. Therefore, it's important to understand the attitudes you each bring with you to your relationship.

The following exercise will help you in this important area.

[NOTE: Hand out Exercise 3.1—one per person. Allow 15 minutes for Exercise 3.1.]

Exercise 3.1

A. Check the main sources from which you received information about sex and sexuality while you were growing up:

___ My parents.

___ Courses in school.
___ Through my church.
___ Through scripture.

___ From watching TV, movies, etc.

___ Teacher, counselor, etc.
___ Former boyfriend/girlfriend.

___ Through Scouts or other organizations.
___ Planned Parenthood.
___ From my friends.
___ From watching how my favorite stars live.
___ Discussions with family doctor.
___ Older brothers and sisters.
___ Locker room discussions.

How has this influenced your behavior? _____

_____

How would you like your own children to learn about sex and sexuality?

_____

_____

Why? _____

B. When it comes to discussing sex and sexuality, which of the following statements would best describe you? (You may check more than one statement.)

___ I am very comfortable discussing sex and sexuality with others.
___ I am comfortable discussing sex and sexuality with my partner.
___ I am eager to learn all I can.
___ I have reverence and awe for the gift of sexuality.
___ Sex is something private which good people don't discuss.
___ I am eager for our marriage to begin so we can explore this whole area more fully.
___ My attitudes may be warped, but I enjoy them.
___ I feel pressured by the whole issue.
___ I don't believe there's anything for me to learn.
___ I'd rather not talk about it.
___ I know I will never change my attitudes.
___ This is a very difficult area for me to talk about.
___ Other_____

Why? _____

C. When I hear the word "sex," I think of... (Check all that apply.)

___	Tenderness	___	Trust	___	Terror
___	Affection	___	Babies	___	Lust
___	Fear	___	Joy	___	Disgust
___	Sleep	___	Birth control	___	Cuddling
___	New techniques	___	Playfulness	___	Orgasm
___	Belonging	___	Faithfulness	___	Wonder
___	Commitment	___	Being used	___	God
___	Giving myself to you	___	Bad memories	___	Romance
___	Satisfaction	___	Dirty jokes	___	Marriage
___	Pornography	___	Communication	___	Reverence

D. In the home where I grew up, the sexual atmosphere was generally... (Check all that apply.)

___	Non-existent	___	Affectionate
___	Open and loving	___	Open but not loving
___	Trusting	___	Caring
___	Healthy	___	Unhealthy
___	Closed	___	Tense
___	Abusive	___	Free and easy
___	Other_____		

E. When we marry, the sexual atmosphere I would like to have between us in our home is:

_____

_____

Why? _____

_____

[Discuss each set of answers with your partner. Focus not only on the answers, but on *why* your partner answered in that way. Really reach for understanding. Can you live with your partner's attitudes for the rest of your life? If change is needed, what change would you like to see take place?]

[NOTE: Allow 15 minutes for Exercise 3.1. Tell the couples when to return. Then proceed with the presentation.]

IV. We find reference to marriage in the very first book of the Old Testament.

[You may read directly from the Bible, Genesis 2:18-25, or from the passage below.]

"Then the Lord God said, 'It is not good that the man should be alone; I will make him a helper as his partner.' So out of the ground the Lord God formed every animal of the fields and every bird of the air, and brought them to the man to see what he would call them; and whatever the man called every living creature, that was its name. The man gave names to all cattle, and to the birds of the air, and to every animal of the field; but for the man there was not found a helper as his partner. So the Lord God caused a deep sleep to fall upon the man, and he slept; then he took one of his ribs and closed up its place with flesh. And the rib that the Lord God had taken from the man he made into a woman and brought her to the man. Then the man said,

> 'This at last is bone of my bones
> and flesh of my flesh;
> This one shall be called Woman
> for out of Man this one was taken.'

"Therefore a man leaves his father and his mother and clings to his wife, and they become one flesh. And the man and his wife were both naked, and were not ashamed."

A. To be fully human, we need to be in relationship to one another. All the gifts of nature were not sufficient to end Adam's loneliness. He needed one like himself with whom he could be in relationship—not as superior and inferior, but in mutuality and interdependence.

B. Creation of woman from the man's rib shows not woman's inferiority, but the natural affinity man and woman have for one another. The joy in this affinity is expressed in Adam's jubilant cry, "This at last is bone of my bones and flesh of my flesh."

C. Sexuality is not considered as evil, but as a God-given gift that draws a man and woman together so they become "one flesh."

D. When this oneness takes place in the commitment of Christian marriage, we leave behind all others, even the members of our own families, and belong totally to one another.

1. This does not mean we have no obligation to our families, but it does mean that in marriage we are to make one another the first priority.
2. When our children arrive, the center of the home and heart of the family is still the couple's love for one another.

E. Adam and Eve are unashamedly naked—a symbol that they were guiltless in their relationship with God and each other. It's this same innocence that we strive for.

F. While the story of Adam and Eve reflects the beauty with which God created us, the Song of Solomon celebrates the passion to which we are called to one another in marriage.

[NOTE: You may read directly from scripture, Song of Solomon 8:6-7, or use the passage below.]

> Set me as a seal upon your heart,
>   as a seal upon your arm;
> for love is strong as death,
>   passion fierce as the grave.
> Its flashes are flashes of fire,
>   a raging flame.
> Many waters cannot quench love,
>   neither can floods drown it.
> If one offered for love
>   all the wealth of his house,
>   it would be utterly scorned.

G. Too often in life, we settle for so much less than God has in mind for us.

1. The Christian marriage relationship is to be passionate and sexual.
2. Too often we see couples live more like a good brother and sister rather than passionate lovers. We call it "settling down."
3. Think about it for a moment. If your brother or sister were to come to live with you, what would you expect of that relationship?

   a. Most likely you would want him/her to be thoughtful and considerate, to help out around the house, to let you know if he/she can't be home on time or be available for dinner, and to occasionally go out with you to dinner, the movies or some other event.
   b. That's a good relationship, but it's not Christian marriage.

4. By its very nature, Christian marriage is both sexual and passionate. It is focused intensely on the other. It should include all of the things listed above, but it includes so much more—our passionate desire for one another that grows over time, not diminishes.
5. This doesn't mean we'll be having sex all the time. It does mean that we will continually choose to focus on the goodness and beauty of the other person, that we will praise and affirm the other, that we will be grateful to God for the gift of one another and we will desire one another passionately. Our love is to grow more intense.

V. When our sexual relationship is no more than an activity something we do with one another to feel good or satisfy ourselves it loses its focus and becomes boring and repetitious.

A. We might refer to our sexual relationship as "it"—and we'll either do "it" or fail to do "it" depending on our mood, our degree of tiredness, or the other distractions in our life.

B. We speak of our "sex life" as though it were something apart from our regular life.

C. We set up unwritten rules for how we'll live out our "sex life." Here are some typical rules.

    1. We'll never do "it" with the lights on.
    2. We'll only do "it" in the bedroom.
    3. We'll never do "it" when the children are up.
    4. We'll never do "it" when visiting or when others are visiting us.
    5. We won't do "it" after the bed has been made.
    6. We'll only do "it" after we've showered.
    7. We'll only do "it" at bedtime—if we're both in the mood.

D. We make up rules to control the behavior of our spouse. The rules come from fear—fear that the other person will be irresponsible or insensitive.

    1. Often, but not always, the rule-maker is the wife. She makes the rules because she believes her husband is irresponsible or doesn't listen to her.
    2. She may also believe her husband is always satisfied in sex and always ready for sex—which may not be the case.
    3. The rules convey the message, "I find you very resistible. You aren't that necessary in my life."
    4. Irresponsibility says, "I want you to satisfy *my* needs; I'm not really interested in yours." "I'm not listening to you."
    5. Both sentiments convey an attitude of superiority toward the other. "If only you were more like me, things would be better."

E. In order to break the impasse, husband and wife must communicate often about all aspects of their sexual relationship — both verbally and non-verbally.

F. Take another look now at more of the attitudes and expectations about sex and sexuality you bring with you into marriage.

G. Even if you've never experienced sexual intercourse, most people bring strong beliefs into marriage with them, and you should be discussing them with each other.

H. You might feel defensive in this area. Please don't pressure each other; just listen and try to understand. Be fully honest and compassionate with each other.

[NOTE: Hand out Exercise 3.2—one per person. Allow 15 minutes for Exercise 3.2.]

Exercise 3.2

Go through the list below and check all the statements with which you agree. Put a * next to all the statements with which you *strongly disagree.*

____ I believe sex must be spontaneous to be good.
____ We should set a romantic mood before we make love.
____ Having sex regularly is a duty.
____ Men enjoy sex more than women do.
____ It's the woman's duty to be responsible for birth control.
____ There's no sense in making love if we don't feel close.
____ Sex will never be an issue in our relationship.
____ It's not possible to go for a period of time without having sex with each other.
____ Sexual intercourse is not a subject nice people discuss.
____ Men can never have sex often enough.
____ If sex is to be good, we both should reach climax.
____ Sex makes a man feel "macho."
____ I think it's important to invite God to be a part of our sexual relationship.
____ The primary purpose of sex is to have children.
____ It's not important how frequently we make love.
____ Planning to make love can take all the joy out of it.
____ The man is basically in charge of the sexual relationship.
____ Married sex can never be as exciting as sex outside of marriage.
____ Men know more about sex than women do.
____ When we make love, it's best to focus on our own pleasure and not our spouse's.
____ I can say "no" to sex anytime I wish.
____ Having a good sexual relationship will keep us faithful to each other.
____ Sex with the same person all your life can get to be boring.
____ If we can't make love for some period of time due to pregnancy, illness, travel, military service, etc., I will remain faithful to you.
____ Pornographic films and magazines will help our sexual relationship.
____ Sex is not all that important to marriage.
____ My partner needs to change his/her attitudes about sex.
____ I believe we need outside help (counseling) in this area.
____ I'm afraid that previous experience will affect the way we relate to one another.
____ I would like to trust God with our family planning.
____ I can't believe God has any interest in our sexual relationship.
____ I would like you to give up pornography.

56

_____ I would like you to trust me more in this area of our relationship.

When do we talk with each other about sex and sexuality? (Check all that apply.)

_____ We seldom or never talk about it.
_____ When a problem arises.
_____ When I'm in a romantic mood.
_____ When you're in a romantic mood.
_____ When we feel trusting with one another.
_____ When we want to change one another.
_____ When we want to learn more about each other.
_____ When we are frustrated with each other.
_____ When we're arguing and want to hurt each other.
_____ When we're looking forward to what it'll be like when we're married.
_____ Other_____

What holds me back from talking more with you about our sexual relationship?

_____ Fear of offending you.   _____ Don't want to argue.
_____ Fear of turning you on.   _____ We have no time to talk.
_____ It's not proper to talk about it.
_____ We're usually too tired to talk.
_____ We're too busy to talk.
_____ I'm embarrassed to talk about it.
_____ I don't want to rock the boat.
_____ I figure we can work it all out later after we're married.
_____ We discuss sex and sexuality regularly.
_____ We have achieved perfect understanding and acceptance of one
      another's views.
_____ I don't want to be criticized.
_____ I sense you don't want to talk about it.
_____ I'm afraid you'll ask me to change.
_____ I'm uncomfortable with some of your attitudes but don't want to hurt
      you by bringing them up.
_____ I don't see the need to talk.
_____ I don't want you to know how ignorant I am about it.
_____ Other_____

[Exchange your answers with your fiancé and go over them, one section at a time. Be sure to listen attentively to one another. Ask questions. Find out why your fiancé answered as he/she did. Make sure you really understand one another. If changes need to be made, make plans for how those changes will begin now before you are married. Include going for professional counseling.]

[NOTE: Allow 15-20 minutes for couples to do this exercise. Tell them when to return. Then resume the presentation.]

Wrap Up

Pornographic movies do not add to the quality of our sexual relationship. In such movies men and women are both degraded. Through their influence our spouse becomes no more than a body to use for our satisfaction. Pornography always distorts our sexuality.

When sex is an activity, it can become routine. We make love on schedule—every Tuesday and Saturday night. We read the public opinion polls and compare ourselves to other couples our age, with our education, and in our socio-economic bracket, to see how often others are doing "it." We put pressure on each other and focus on method and technique. We may become more competent, but are less passionate.

We lose our sense of wonder about each other. Sexual intercourse is no longer a wonderful gift from God that we build toward all day long. Instead, it's what we do when we go to bed at night, when we're totally exhausted and neither of us wants to put much effort into it.

When we use sex only as an activity, withholding sex can be our way of punishing our partner. Or demanding sex whenever we want it, without regard for our partner, can be a power play. Such power plays are signs of insecure persons. When sex is no more than an activity, we are robbing ourselves of all the joy and intimacy God wants us to share in marriage. Making love is not *something we do*, it's *who we are* to one another. Just as we can decide to make love, we can decide to work at being in love twenty-four hours a day. That calls for responsibility, sensitivity and attentiveness on both our parts.

VI. In every marriage, there is often an unspoken desire for control.

A. *No Power:* One partner often takes control of the sexual relationship, while the other controls communications.

1. We generally believe this to be the person who initiates sex—the one who says, either verbally or non-verbally, "Let's make love tonight."
2. The person who is really in control, however, is the one who has the power to say, "Yes, we will," or "No, we won't."
3. In every marriage, one person also has control of how well and how frequently the couple will communicate with one another—how often they'll have intimate conversation.
4. We may believe the one who has this power is the one who says, "We've got to talk," or "I wish you'd just listen to me."
5. But the one who has real power over communications is the one who says, "Yes, we will talk," or "No, I won't."

58

B. In most (but not all) marriages, it is the woman who is in control of the sexual relationship and the man who is in control of their conversation.

C. God invites us to enter into a relationship defined by mutuality, where we each give up power over the other, where we are mutually submissive to one another.

D. *Parallels Between Intimate Conversation and Sexual Intimacy*

1. In every marriage, there is deep need for both good verbal communication and a strong sexual relationship.
2. Without both, there is a sense of resentment on the part of one or the other, a feeling of being cheated of something.
3. When a wife lets her husband know she is not interested in him sexually (either by telling him or by simply avoiding him), she may simply be stating, "I don't feel like *it*," or "I'm too tired to do *it*."
4. But what he hears is, "I'm not interested in *you* tonight. I don't want *you*." He takes it as a personal rejection of him.
5. When a husband tells his wife he's not interested in talking with her, he may simply be saying, "I'm tired. I've worked hard all day and I just want to be left alone."
6. But what she hears is, "I'm not interested in *you* or how you feel. I don't care about *you*." She takes it as a personal rejection of her.

E. Summary: Remember how we discussed focusing on the other person in the talk on communications earlier today?

1. We are called to give up our focus on self in marriage and to focus on one another and our relationship.
2. Sometimes we'll make love when one of us doesn't feel like it and we'll have intimate talks when one of us would rather be doing something else.
3. Then we can ask God to send us the grace we need to be caring and attentive at that moment.

F. When we simply are too tired, too sick or too distracted to focus on one another either in conversation or love-making, then we should explain with gentleness and love—and set a time for when we will make love or talk. We can make a definite date for sometime within the next twenty-four hours.

1. In this way, our beloved will know that he/she is still deeply loved and it's only with regret that we have to postpone our time together.
2. Sexual intercourse does not have to be *spontaneous* in order to be exciting and fulfilling.

G. Continue to show the same thoughtfulness you have for one another today throughout your marriage together.

VII. Sex as Communication

A. Sexual intercourse is the most powerful form of non-verbal communication between a husband and wife.

B. When a man and woman make love, a powerful bond forms between them —a bond that turns them toward one another rather than away.

1. They tend to be more attentive to one another, to listen better, to be more affectionate and gentle with each other.
2. Even two strong, independent people are more likely to give up some of that independence and allow the other person to influence them.
3. Making love tends to "gentle us down."

C. The passionate love of a man and woman in Christian marriage is so much more than duty, responsibility, or activity. It is a relationship that is total, giving, creative, committed, enthusiastic, and hopeful.

D. Let's take a look at what sexual intercourse communicates:

1. Sometimes in making love, the couple communicate their *feelings of celebration.* They've just had a great day, a romantic evening, or a special occasion. You just got a raise, and it's time to celebrate.
2. Sometimes love-making communicates *support for one another.* When one of you has had a terrible day at work or you've just lost your job or have been heavily criticized, making love says to the person, "I believe in you. No matter what happens, I will always love you."
3. *When our self-image* is low and we notice we've gained weight, or we're getting gray or wrinkled, making love can say, "I think you're irresistible. To me you are always beautiful."
4. Hurt feelings can remain after an argument is settled, but you can decide to make love even though you don't feel like it. Then *love-making soothes away the bitter feelings* that may linger, the harsh judgments, or the hidden belief, "I know I was right." Love-making communicates, "No issue is so great that it will ever divide us. We may not know how to solve this problem at this time, but together we will always work out our problems."
5. Finally, *love-making is healing.* In times of pain and deep emotional crisis, such as the death of a loved one, the married couple's love-making draws them out of the pain, into the loving reality of each other's arms. Then love-making communicates, "I share with you this grief and sorrow. I will never leave you to face your grief alone."

VIII. Married couples should plan their love-making together and not leave it to chance or to when they both feel like it.

A. Make love in prime time—not when you're both exhausted and have little to offer one another.

B. Spend time together just touching and holding each other without making love. Enjoy the beauty and gift of the other person.

C. Be affectionate and thoughtful throughout the day. Don't expect to jump into bed and "turn on."

D. You don't have to feel like making love in order to make love. Sometimes you won't feel like it, but your husband/wife needs you. Often, once you've begun, you'll start to feel good about it.

E. Always say "yes" to the person, even if you have to say "no" to the action. Make your lives a total "yes" to one other.

F. Be sensitive and caring. Set aside time for just the two of you on a regular, even daily basis.

IX. Sex and sexuality in God's eyes is a gift meant to be used wisely and well by his people.

A. There is a twofold purpose for sexual intercourse.

1. It is a gift that gives new life to the couple in their relationship.
2. It also brings new life into the world in our babies and children.

B. God intended for men and women to be co-creators with him—to share in the great gift of bringing life into the world.

C. He did this by conferring on husband and wife a love so powerful that it has to have a name—the name you give your child.

D. In some ways, you could say that each child is an outward sign of your love for one another—of the way you loved each other at that time.

E. Just as in all other moral decisions, each couple decides for themselves, in the total context of their lives, when to accept this possibility of having a child. This must be a fully informed decision, and there are a number of issues to be considered.

* * * * *

[NOTE: Catholic Insert (If this is not used as a Catholic program, you *may use your own discretion about which part of the insert to use or skip it altogether.)*

The Catholic teaching is that couples must be open to the dual purposes of sexual intercourse: bringing new life and love into the couple's own relationship and bringing new life into the world in their children.

A. If a couple is unable to conceive, there is no burden placed on them by the church.

B. However, if a couple can conceive and chooses to never have children, this is considered an impediment to marriage.

C. Such couples should discuss their individual situations with the priest who will witness their wedding ceremony.

The Catholic Church accepts natural family planning as a means to space children when there are serious reasons why a couple cannot conceive at a certain point in their marriage (illness, poverty, loss of job, emotional incapacity, etc.). Most priests are well equipped to discuss these issues individually with the couples as the need arises, and they should not be afraid to approach a priest.

Natural family planning is not the same as the old rhythm method that was used years ago. It is much more accurate and does involve the natural rhythms of the woman's cycle to measure her days of fertility.

A. It includes several days of abstinence from sexual intercourse (on their fertile days) each month.

B. It has the advantage that it is completely natural and involves both partners equally.

C. The disadvantage is that some couples fear that abstinence is not possible for them.

D. Further information can be found (Identify where they can learn more about natural family planning.)]

* * * * *

E. You are the only ones who can decide how many children you will have. The ability to bring new life into the world and to nurture the lives of children is a gift from God. It is a source of great joy and great responsibility. Take the time you need, as often as you need, to discuss and pray about your decisions. You may want to meet with your pastor to discuss the issues, and invite the pastor to add his/her insights to your discussion.

F. Conclusion

1. When a married couple is passionately in love with one another, their world and the world of those they touch is a much better place.
2. The entire atmosphere of the home is transformed when the love of the couple for each other and for God is at its center.
3. God blesses our sex and sexuality. It is a gift to be used wisely and well; it is a gift that brings joy and peace, not only to the couple, but to the family and community as well.
4. Throughout time, man and woman have been meant by God to bring life to one another and the earth in order that life may then return again to God. The relationship between a man and a woman is meant to be one of partnership in giving glory to God.

We have another exercise for you.

[NOTE: Hand out one copy per person of Exercise 3.3. Allow 20 minutes to complete it.]

Exercise 3.3

Below are a number of possible attitudes about having a family. Put a check mark next to each statement which you believe describes your attitude.

____ The commitment to marriage includes the decision to be open to new life. It's a decision I want to discuss now and regularly throughout our marriage.

____ Any decision to postpone a family should be made only on a temporary basis. It should be a topic that can be reopened at any time by either of us.

____ Sometimes when couples marry, they both plan to continue full-time with their careers. After the arrival of the first child, however, one of them may decide to remain at home. Sometimes the other partner then feels cheated because he/she was counting on the extra income. These are decisions we'll discuss often and seriously.

____ I agree with the research that indicates children benefit greatly when they are cared for by their own parents.

____ I view children as a burden who will cramp our lifestyle.

____ Children are a gift from God, a special source of joy and delight. They are also a call to spiritual and emotional growth as we learn the true meaning of selflessness and giving of ourselves to others.

____ A decision about the number of children we'll have should be thoughtfully and prayerfully considered.

____ If we choose not to conceive a child at any particular point, it will be an occasion of regret for me.

____ I do not plan to have children in this marriage.

___ If we are unable to conceive our own children easily, I would go to extra-ordinary means to conceive a child.
___ I would be willing to adopt a child.
___ If we were to be infertile, I would be deeply upset.

Now share your responses with your partner and discuss them with each other.

When it comes to having babies, I am the type of person who would... (Check all that apply.)

___ Want to have as many as possible.
___ Be very nervous about the whole thing.
___ Be concerned about our finances.
___ Look forward to playing with them.
___ Worry about who was going to take care of them.
___ Plan the whole thing very carefully.
___ Tell all my friends immediately.
___ Trust God to be with us.
___ Be horrified just thinking about it.
___ Take on a second job or work overtime to support them.
___ Start planning immediately for their college education.
___ Take one day at a time.
___ *Never* agree to an abortion.
___ Other_____

I think the ideal time for us to start a family is _____

Now that I realize that we need both intimate conversation as well as sexual intimacy, I feel...

_____

_____

How can I make my life a total "yes" to you?

_____

_____

When you have both finished writing your responses, read one another's answers and discuss them in some detail. Make sure you fully understand and *agree with* what your partner is saying to you. If it's not possible to reach agreement, you may want to discuss this issue further with your pastor.

[NOTE: Allow 15 minutes for the exercise. Then close the session. You may want to take a short break before the next session.]

Session Four
*The Covenant of Marriage**
(Scripture: 1 John 4:7-12
and Ephesians 5:21-33)

[NOTE: One team member begins with a prayer.]

Prayer

Pray for openness to God's plan for us. Mention any barriers you or the participants may have to being completely open and trusting with God—for example, fear of the future, fear of giving up control of my life, having no personal relationship with God, not really trusting God, etc.

I. In order to get our thoughts together for the next presentation, it may be helpful to stop for a few moments to reflect on our relationship with the church and what we hope for by marrying in the church.

A. This is just a brief exercise to help you clarify your thoughts.

B. As usual, you won't be asked to share your answers with anyone except your partner, so please be honest in your answers with one another.

[NOTE: Hand out a copy of Exercise 4.1 to each person. Allow 15 minutes for the exercise. Then resume the presentation. They may stay in their places for this exercise.]

*In the Catholic program and in some Christian programs, you may wish to change the wording to Sacrament of Matrimony.

Exercise 4.1

A. You have come to the church to witness your commitment to marry one another. Why have you chosen to have your wedding witnessed by the church? (Check all that apply.)

____ It's traditional in our family to "marry" in church.
____ I have a profound faith in God.
____ The church building provides a beautiful setting.
____ My mother/father wants us to be married in church.
____ My partner's mother/father wants us to be married in church.
____ This church was a compromise for both of us.
____ I grew up in this church/this denomination.
____ I have a strong sense of belonging to this church.
____ My partner wanted a church wedding.
____ It feels right to make a permanent commitment in the presence of God.
____ Other_____

(What other reasons would you add for why you have chosen a church wedding?)

B. When it comes to making a permanent lifelong commitment to love someone, I'm the kind of person who would say (check YES or NO to each statement):

YES NO

____ ____ This is an easy thing for me to do.
____ ____ This really scares me.
____ ____ I'll try this, but if it doesn't work, I want to get out of it.
____ ____ I really want God to bless this commitment.
____ ____ I'm putting all my trust in God to help us.
____ ____ I hope I never have to work at this relationship.
____ ____ If times get difficult between us, I'm willing to go for counseling.
____ ____ I hope we always grow more and more in love, and I'm willing to work hard to make that happen.
____ ____ Enrichment programs for married couples might be something that would interest me.
____ ____ This commitment applies now, but if I continue to grow and change, it may not apply in the future.
____ ____ I'm not sure it's possible to love someone for a lifetime.
____ ____ I'm willing to change my priorities in order to make our marriage work.
____ ____ Other_____

(What other things would you say about your permanent commitment to one another?)

C. What do you hope to gain from the church community? (Check all that apply.)

___ Nothing, really.
___ We simply want to use the church and have a minister preside.
___ We belong to this community.
___ We would consider belonging to this community.
___ We live out of town, but this community represents our own community where we live.
___ The church community speaks to me of God's love for me/us.
___ The marriage covenant is a private commitment. The church community has nothing to do with it.
___ Other—_____

(What additional expectations do you have for this faith community you have chosen for your wedding?)

[Share your answers with your partner. Make sure you understand clearly what the other person is saying. If the other person does not share your views on certain questions, find out why he/she chose that particular answer.]

[NOTE: Allow 10 minutes for this exercise. Then resume the presentation.]

Wrap Up

I. When a couple comes to the church for their marriage, they are implying that God is important in their lives.

A. They want their marriage to be blessed by God.

B. They wish to be married in the presence of God and God's witnesses.

C. They desire to have God in their relationship, not just on their wedding day, but in all the days and years that lie ahead.

II. For some engaged couples, the focus is not on God, but only on their plans for a beautiful wedding and a lovely reception and honeymoon.

A. The fact that you have chosen to come to the church for your marriage is symbolic of the religious training and background either or both of you may share and of your desire to get your marriage off to the best possible start.

B. The fact that you're willing to participate in a marriage preparation day such as this indicates your willingness to be open to one another and to

God—to literally allow the other to enter into you and form your mind and heart.

C. These are all positive, wonderful signs about the seriousness with which you make this commitment to marriage as well as your trust in God to help you keep your commitment.

D. Whether we are aware of it or not, when we are open to lifelong committed love, we are also open to God's love.

E. Listen to what we read in scripture from 1 John 4:7-12:

[NOTE: Read these verses directly from a Bible.]

"Beloved, let us love one another, because love is from God; everyone who loves is born of God and knows God. Whoever does not love does not know God, for God is love. God's love was revealed among us in this way: God sent his only Son into the world so that we might live through him. In this is love, not that we loved God but that he loved us and sent his Son to be the atoning sacrifice for our sins. Beloved, since God loved us so much, we also ought to love one another. No one has ever seen God; if we love one another, God lives in us, and his love is perfected in us."

1. God loves us so much, he sent his Son to us to show us how to live in love with one another and to teach us to be merciful in our love.

2. When Jesus came, he revealed his Father as total love.

3. Few people will experience God's love directly in mystical visions, inner voices, or insights. The way most people experience God's love, compassion, forgiveness, and understanding is in the love we share with one another, especially in marriage and family.

4. When we live in love with one another, we not only fulfill God's command to love one another, but we also make God's love come alive here on earth.

5. Love originates in God and goes out through us to one another. In Christian marriage we have an awesome and wonderful responsibility.

III. Experiencing God

A. Since God is the essence of love and at the heart of what we are all about as a couple, it is essential to understand how each of us knows and experiences God in our own lives.

B. It's also important to know what to expect from one another in the years ahead about how each plans to grow in love and knowledge of God.

C. Exercise 4.2 will help us focus on some of these questions.

[NOTE: Hand out Exercise 4.2—one per person. If necessary, go over the directions to make sure all participants understand what they are to do. Allow them about 15 minutes to write their answers and to share as a couple.]

Exercise 4.2

A. When you think of God, what images come to your mind? (Check all that apply.)

___	Wise old man.	___	Harsh judge.
___	Scorekeeper of good and evil.	___	A mother figure.
___	The ten commandments.	___	A father figure.
___	A Being of total love.	___	Creator of all.
___	One who inspires love in me.		
___	One who inspires fear in me.		
___	I don't believe in God.		
___	I've never really thought about God.		
___	I'd like to know more about God.		
___	Other_____		

(In what other ways would you describe God or your relationship to him?)

B. The following are words that have sometimes been used to describe Jesus. How would you describe Jesus? (Check all that apply.)

___	Gentle	___	Kind
___	Compassionate	___	A healer
___	Our Savior	___	The crucified
___	Redeemer	___	Demanding
___	My personal Savior	___	A friend
___	A brother	___	A trouble-maker
___	The Messiah	___	A prophet
___	A stranger to me	___	Not important to me
___	Challenging	___	Teacher
___	I have a personal relationship with Jesus.		
___	I don't feel close to Jesus.		
___	I don't know much about Jesus or his teachings.		
___	I want to know more about Jesus.		
___	I don't believe in Jesus.		
___	Other_____		

(In what other ways would you describe Jesus or your relationship to him?)

C. The following is a list of religious attitudes and practices. Go through the list and check off all those that apply to you. Put a * next to those that are *most important* to you.

____   I believe going to church every Sunday is important for us.

____   I want to make God the center of our home and our love.

____   I believe it is important to have outward signs of our faith in our home (a cross or other religious symbols). The most significant religious symbol to me is _____.

     I would like to have this symbol in our home. ___ Yes ___ No

____   I believe it's important to pray every day.

____   I plan to pray every day.

____   I would like us to pray together.

     How often? _____

____   I believe that if we say we love God, we must also keep his commands.

____   I believe in God, but I don't believe any particular religious practice is necessary.

____   I don't believe in God and don't intend to practice any religion.

____   I'm angry with God.

____   I enjoy spiritual reading (i.e. Christian books, magazines, journals, etc.)

____   I would like you to continue to practice your faith after we are married.

____   I would eventually like us to become members of the same faith community.

____   I believe all things are God's gifts to us.

____   I believe God knows and loves each of us intimately.

____   I believe knowing and understanding the Bible is important.

____   I would like to attend Bible study classes after we are married.

     ___ Yes ___ No

____   I find God's presence everywhere.

____   I believe God helped us find each other.

____   I believe God blesses our love.

____   As a child I studied religion.

____   I want our children to study religion.

____   I believe baptism is important.

____   I want our children to be baptized.

     In what faith community? _____

____   I believe there is life after death.

____   I hope to spend eternity with God in heaven.

____   I don't believe in life after death.

____   I believe it is important to have friends with whom we can share our faith.

____   I believe that if we are really living our faith, we probably won't always fit in with what others are doing in our society.

____   I believe it is important to avoid doing things which may hurt someone else or myself.

___ I believe we are called to forgive those who hurt us.

___ I try to forgive everyone who has hurt me.

___ I believe God will help us overcome any temptations that would destroy our marriage.

___ I believe we can make God's love real to one another.

___ I believe we can help one another get to heaven.

___ I believe it is important to be involved in church activities beyond Sunday services.

___ I will teach our children to pray and pray with them.

___ I will respect your religious beliefs and encourage you to practice your faith.

___ I will help you find time to pray each day.

___ I am willing to continue to talk to you about our religious beliefs.

___ I am willing to respect any differences we may have in our beliefs.

___ I will avoid any sense of religious superiority over you.

[Share your answers with one another. Take your time and go over them carefully—listening with your heart. If you wish, begin your discussion with a prayer and invite God to be with you as you discuss this most intimate part of your lives together.]

[*NOTE: Allow 15 minutes for this exercise. Then resume the talk.*]

Wrap Up

A. For many couples, their relationship with God is a powerful bond that unites them even when they run into difficulties or experience great sorrow or suffering.

B. In fact, with couples who have deep faith, their suffering can draw them closer to God and to one another.

C. For others, their religious beliefs are a difficult topic; they seldom or never discuss them.

   1. As a result, they often experience loneliness and misunderstanding in this area.

   2. One may pray and practice a religious faith, while the other slips away from any involvement. One may be forced to become the spiritual head of the household, responsible for the spiritual needs of the entire family. This can lead to great resentment.

   3. For some, religious practices are such a hot topic that they refuse to discuss the issue. They're afraid of rocking the boat.

71

a. Sometimes this leads to religious indifference on both persons' part.

b. They practice no religion, seldom or never pray, do not read the Bible, and live only for the moment. But this is like burying your head in the sand.

c. Sooner or later every person has to face the issues of life and death.

4. How we see and experience God greatly influences the way we will respond to all our difficulties and challenges in life.

5. We must talk about our relationship with God and church and work toward unity as much as possible—understanding our differences and emphasizing our similarities.

6. Through our prayer we will open ourselves to God's grace which we need to grow in faith and oneness.

IV. The Covenant of Marriage

A. In Ephesians 5:21-33, we have another description of marriage—one that has caused some concern among couples today who are reacting to abuse in relationships in our society. But, nevertheless, these words from scripture offer a viewpoint from a Christian perspective that still holds valuable insights for us.

B. [NOTE: Read Ephesians 5:21-33. Read directly from Bible if available.]

> "Be subject to one another out of reverence for Christ.
>
> "Wives, be subject to your husbands as you are to the Lord. For the husband is the head of the wife just as Christ is the head of the church, the body of which he is the Savior. Just as the church is subject to Christ, so also wives ought to be, in everything, to their husbands.
>
> "Husbands, love your wives, just as Christ loved the church and gave himself up for her, in order to make her holy by cleansing her with the washing of water by the word, so as to present the church to himself in splendor, without a spot or wrinkle or anything of the kind—yes, so that she may be holy and without blemish. In the same way, husbands should love their wives as they do their own bodies. He who loves his wife loves himself. For no one ever hates his own body, but he nourishes and tenderly cares for it, just as Christ does for the church, because we are members of his body. For this reason a man will leave his father and mother and be joined to his wife, and the two will become one flesh. This is a great mystery, and I am applying it to Christ and the church. Each of you, however, should love his wife as himself, and a wife should respect her husband."

C. St. Paul tells us that our baptism makes each of us a member of the body of Christ.

1. As members of that body, we are called to a mutual submission to one another—not that we give up our individuality or lose our personality,

but that we respect, cherish and honor each other. We are invited to enter into a profound bond of trust—trust in God and trust in one another. When we commit ourselves to this kind of trust, there is no one superior. This is the kind of equality between men and women that the world is searching for.

2. A Christian marriage invites us to enter into the mystery of Christ's love—a love so rich and so passionate that he was willing to die for us.

3. While most of us will never be asked to die for our beloved, we will often have to die to ourselves, our self-will, our selfishness, in order to consider the good of the other and of our relationship.

4. We are not talking about giving up or giving in; we are simply talking about total giving of ourselves to one another.

5. The cross is a rich and powerful symbol of God's love for us. It is also a powerful symbol of married love. We will be one another's greatest blessing and also one another's greatest cross.

D. St. Paul tells us that in a Christian marriage the couple's witness of their love for one another becomes a sign of how much Christ loves the church.

1. We can't actually see Jesus' love — his spiritual union with each one of us.

2. However, we can see the love of a man and a woman for one another. We can experience it, be part of it, enjoy it, and bask in the warmth of a love that grows stronger day by day, month by month and year by year.

3. It's not the unrealistic love of two unreal, perfect people who never have an argument or disagreement between them, but the love of real, imperfect, people who are willing to understand one another's short-comings and work on *changing themselves* to be considerate of the other and grow toward perfection in the eyes of God.

4. The process of living out a Christian marriage is much more than just fulfilling a number of obligations. It involves taking the person I love and making him/her part of my very identity.

   a. It means that my spouse will be my first priority—above all others, including the members of my own family.

   b. I will take your feelings, your values, your ideas into consideration before I make any decisions.

   c. On a practical level this will include everything from the type of coffee we'll put in the coffeemaker every morning, to whether or not we'll accept an out-of-town job, to where we'll have our next holiday dinner.

5. By our baptism we are called to be agents of God's love in many ways. Through our married love, we will bring God's love not only to one

another, but to the entire faith community—as well as those with whom we live and work.

E. This is the covenant of Christian marriage. It is a commitment of the couple to each other and to the Christian community to love one another forever and to work on their relationship throughout their lives "in good times and in bad," to represent their faith community through the witness of their married love.

1. It is also a commitment of the faith community to love and support the married couple throughout their lives in whatever way the couple needs assistance, "in good times and in bad."
2. Both the faith community and the couple are saying yes to the marriage vows.
3. The couple promises to model the love of Jesus to the whole community. The community promises to model the love of Jesus to the couple.

F. The marriage covenant is much more than a contract. Every contract has conditions that can make it null and void.

1. The covenant made by Jesus Christ has no conditions. It is a total commitment.
2. Since none of us knows what the future has in store, it's frightening to think of entering into such a covenant.
3. That's why we have each other and the whole community. That's why we have our faith in God to love and guide all of us and remain with us throughout our lives.
4. In our marriage covenant, we place ourselves totally in God's hands. God will never fail us.

[NOTE: The presenting couple cites a personal experience as an example of how they have experienced God's love in their marriage or family.]

G. Jesus made many promises to his followers. We don't always experience these promises, but even when things are difficult, and we aren't aware of it, the promises still stand.

H. Let's look at how you and your beloved are already bringing the love of Jesus to one another. We have another exercise for you.

[NOTE: Hand out Exercise 4.3.]

Exercise 4.3

What beautiful qualities does your fiancée share in common with Jesus? How has your fiancée brought Jesus' love alive for you? Go through the list below and put a check mark next to all those qualities of love you have seen in your partner in the time you have known one another.

____ You have always stressed my good qualities. I always feel affirmed by you.

____ You are not critical or judgmental of me.

____ You have always been faithful to me.

____ You have made me your first priority.

____ You brag about me to others.

____ You are not constantly threatening to break up with me.

____ You are enthusiastic in your love for me.

____ You are willing to sit and talk with me—to share your views and ideas and to listen to mine.

____ You are willing to come to days such as this to work at deepening our relationship.

____ You are passionate in your love for me.

____ You are not afraid of intimacy.

____ You never hold a grudge or say, "I told you so."

____ You are quick to forgive me when I have offended you.

____ You have never hit me, insulted me, or called me names.

____ You encourage me to try new things, take new risks because you are at my side.

____ I always feel special when I'm around you.

____ You are very tender and concerned when I don't feel well or I am upset about something.

Now go back through the list and put a * next to your fiancée's strongest quality.

What qualities of Jesus' love do you plan to bring to your beloved in your marriage? (Check all that apply.)

____ I will love you with a passionate, life-giving, and holy love.

____ I will be faithful to you not simply in sexual matters, but I will carry you in my mind and my heart wherever I go.

____ I will make you my first priority—ahead of my friends and even my family.

____ I will brag about your good qualities to others.

____ I will not criticize you to friends.

____ I will praise and affirm you so that you may grow in confidence and self-esteem.

____ I will never threaten you with divorce even when I'm very angry with you.

____ I will love you enthusiastically and show my love for you in all the big and little ways that make you happy.

____ I will work on our relationship every day of my life.

____ If our relationship becomes difficult, I will get counseling or look for help and encourage you to do the same.
____ When I have hurt you, I will ask for your forgiveness.
____ When you ask for forgiveness, I will always grant it to you.
____ As far as I am concerned, this marriage is forever.
____ I won't get into a pattern of blaming you when things go wrong.
____ I will work on keeping our love alive and passionate, just as Jesus was passionate in his love for us.

Go back through the list and put a * next to the quality you feel most strongly about developing.

Now write a love letter to your partner and include the following points:

1. Tell your fiancée of the most beautiful quality you see in him/her. Give some examples of when you have experienced that quality.
2. Write of the quality you plan to develop in your relationship after you are married. Be as specific as possible. Which quality will you develop? How will you do it? What changes are you willing to make in order to accomplish it? If you have time, you may write about more than one quality.
3. Close your love letter with words of love for your partner.

When you have both finished writing, share your responses with your partner.

[NOTE: Allow 15 minutes for this exercise. Since most couples tend to drift back in after finishing this exercise, you will probably not need to take a break.]

Session Five
Going Forth

[NOTE: Have blank paper (one sheet per person) for the evaluation. The evaluation is an optional exercise, meant to be feedback for the team. It is not recommended if you are working in a one-to-one relationship with a couple.]

I. We have some final things to do before we conclude this DAY-BY-DAY workshop. We began the day by asking you to talk to each other about what you hoped to gain today. Now we ask you to spend a few minutes writing your individual response to the question, "How has this workshop affected me?" We're passing out a piece of paper for you to use. Do not put your name on the paper. We'll collect it in a few minutes.

[NOTE: Pass out the blank paper, Exercise 5.1, and give them no more than 5 minutes to write. Collect the evaluations.]

II. In addition to what we covered today, there are many other topics which can lead to fruitful discussion and help you prepare for your marriage.

A. Your pastor can provide you with material that will assist you. We recommend that you ask him for his suggestions.

B. We have a take-home book for you. We strongly recommend that you use the book as a couple. Do the written exercises, and spend some time discussing your responses to each of them. Perhaps you can set aside an hour to go through each one of them.

C. The book is a series of short exercises and covers many topics we didn't have a chance to discuss today such as:

1. When You're Discussing Money...

2. When You're Disappointed in One Another…
3. When You're Having an Argument…
4. When You're Discussing the Roles of Men and Women…
5. When You're Concerned About Your In-Laws…
6. When You're Having an Argument…
7. When Should We Go for Counseling?

D. It also includes summaries of the talks we did today.

[NOTE: Hand out books.]

III. Announcements

[NOTE: You may include any of the following or add your own.

1. Remind the couples to take home all their personal possessions and their exercises from the day.
2. Ask them to help clean up the hall.
3. If you are serving dinner now, announce it.
4. If there's a closing ceremony, announce that.
5. If the next DAY-BY-DAY workshop is scheduled, announce it and ask the couples to tell their friends about it.
6. If you want the couples to have a copy of When To Consider Postponing the Wedding, hand it out at this time.
7. Add any other announcements.]

IV. Closing Prayer

[NOTE: Hand out copies of the closing prayer. Ask the couples to stand and join you in reading aloud the prayer below.]

Loving God, we thank you for the wonderful gift of our love for each other.
Help us every day of our lives to grow more in love with each other and with you.
The urgency and desire we have for each other is only a shadow of the way you love us.
We pray that you will help us to always live as bride and groom and never take each other for granted.
Bless us with wisdom and understanding. Reveal to us where we need to change our behavior in order to make love grow.
Teach us how to forgive each other and to seek forgiveness as soon as we realize we have hurt each other.
Help us to understand that our Christian marriage is rooted in the church and that the people of God will always be at our side to help us love one another.
Send us your Spirit, O Lord, that we may truly see ourselves as an image of Christ's love for his church.
In joy or sorrow, in riches or poverty, in sickness and in health—may our love grow into your divine love till death do us part.
Amen.

Exercises

Exercise 1.1

Put a check mark next to all answers which apply to you. There is a space at the end (Other_____) to write in your own reason if none of the rest apply to you.

A. Why did I come here today?
- __ I love you very much.
- __ I'm willing to go anywhere for you.
- __ I felt forced to come.
- __ I came to learn more about you.
- __ Our pastor told us to come.
- __ I wanted to please you.
- __ I want to give our marriage the best possible start.
- __ Some friends have come and liked it.
- __ I'm not sure why I came.
- __ Other_____

B. What do I hope to gain here today?
- __ Deeper awareness of you.
- __ Increasing love for you.
- __ To learn more about what a Christian marriage is.
- __ Peace of mind.
- __ Insight into myself.
- __ The skills I need for a great marriage.
- __ A few hours to talk with you without distractions.
- __ Answers to some of my questions.
- __ I honestly don't expect to gain anything.
- __ Other_____

[After you finish writing, exchange your answer sheets and share your answers with your future spouse. You can stay right where you are seated and talk softly to each other. Be sure to tell one another *why* you answered as you did. You'll have about 5 minutes to do this.]

Exercise 1.2

A. What would you like your life/your marriage to be like one year from now? (Where will you be living? Will you have children? How will you behave toward one another?)

_____

_____

_____

B. What would you like your life/your marriage to be like ten years from now? (Where will you be living? Will you have children? How will you behave toward one another?)

_____

_____

C. What beautiful qualities of love as mentioned in St. Paul's letter do you see in your beloved? Describe the evidence.

__	Patience	__	Kindness
__	Inner peace	__	Humility
__	Generosity of spirit	__	Tactful
__	Giving	__	Inner joy
__	Forgiving	__	Understanding
__	Compassion	__	Persevering
__	Faithfulness	__	Rejoices in the truth
__	Love of God	__	Deeply caring
__	Other (_____)		

[Put a check mark next to the strongest quality. When do you see that most fully present in your beloved?]

D. When you are seventy years old, how would you like to be able to describe your life and marriage to your grandchildren? What would you have hoped your life together would have been like?

_____

_____

_____

When you finish writing, exchange what you have written and compare your answers with each other. How do you agree? How do you disagree?

A. Below are listed a number of reasons why some people find it difficult to communicate or to talk honestly about their deepest feelings. Go through the list and put a check mark next to every reason why you may find it difficult to share with your partner on at least some areas of your relationship.

ME	MY FIANCÉE	
___	___	I don't know how.
___	___	I didn't know I'd be asked to do this.
___	___	I'm afraid to make you angry.
___	___	I'm not sure I want to get into this.
___	___	I have been hurt before by *someone else*. I'm afraid to trust again.
___	___	I've been hurt before by *you*. I'm afraid to trust again.
___	___	We never have much time to talk without distractions.
___	___	My family never did this.
___	___	None of our friends does this and they seem to be doing all right.
___	___	I don't see myself as a very "deep" person.
___	___	If I tell you everything about me, will you still want to marry me?
___	___	We're usually too tired to talk.
___	___	I don't want to start a fight.
___	___	I'm hoping you'll change after we're married.
___	___	I'm afraid of a broken engagement or postponed wedding.
___	___	I worry about whether we'll be able to work through our differences if we open up a difficult issue.
___	___	Other_____

Now go back through the list and put a check mark next to every reason why you believe your fiancée may hold back in sharing with you, at least in some areas.

Identify an area where you would like to know your fiancée's feelings more clearly.

_____

Identify an area where you would like to explain your feelings more clearly to your fiancée.

_____

B. Below are some stereotypical statements often made about men and women that may or may not be true for the two of you. Go through the list and put a check mark next to each statement you believe is true for you. Men write in the HIS column; women write in the HERS column. Then go back through the list and put a * next to each statement you believe describes your partner.

HIS	HERS	
—	—	Men are directed outward.
—	—	Women are directed inward.
—	—	A man's self-image focuses on "what I do."
—	—	A woman's self-image focuses on "who I am."
—	—	Men tend to be competitive.
—	—	Women tend to value cooperation.
—	—	Men value independence.
—	—	Women value interdependence.
—	—	Women talking to women stress their feelings and emphasize relationships.
—	—	Men talking to men stress external events, what they accomplished, happenings in the world of sports, etc.
—	—	Men don't pay much attention to feelings.
—	—	Women pay a lot of attention to sharing of feelings.
—	—	Men tend to be goal-oriented. "We made that decision. Let's move on to something else."
—	—	Women tend to be process-oriented. "I've changed my mind. I want to discuss that decision again."
—	—	Women are more likely to press for good communications than men.

Take a few minutes to share your answers with one another.

Exercise 2.2

A. Below are a series of statements about your family-of-origin and how they communicated with one another. On the left hand side, under the column *MY FAMILY*, check all those statements that apply to your family-of-origin. If you grew up in more than one home, or were adopted, choose the answers which applied most of the time. On the right hand side, under the column *OUR MARRIAGE*, put a check mark after each statement you want to put into practice *in your own home*.

MY FAMILY		OUR MARRIAGE
___	We never lied to one another.	___
___	We were always able to express feelings honestly.	___
___	We were never too tired or too preoccupied to listen.	___
___	We often only partially listened to each other.	___
___	We didn't make snap judgments about the other person.	___
___	We often spoke before the other finished talking.	___
___	We often shouted, pounded a fist, or waved our arms to make a point.	___
___	We always faced up to our differences.	___
___	We complimented one another often.	___
___	We always looked for the goodness in one another.	___
___	Criticism was a regular part of life.	___
___	We called each other names.	___
___	We did much good-natured teasing.	___
___	We laughed a great deal and had fun together.	___
___	One member of the family was always tense or defensive.	___
___	We thought shouting helped us make our point.	___
___	Slamming a door or leaving the house was often part of an argument.	___
___	Some family members stopped speaking to each other rather than argue.	___
___	Not speaking to each other is a regular form of punishment in my family.	___
___	We turned off TV/radio or put down a newspaper to pay attention to each other.	___
___	We made time to be together just to enjoy one another's company.	___
___	My parents kept secrets from each other.	___
___	Only weak people cried in front of each other.	___
___	We were openly affectionate with one another.	___
___	My parents often had intimate talks together.	___
___	Forgiveness was a normal part of making up.	___
___	There were no "winners" or "losers" in an argument.	___
___	When angry, it was permissible to sulk and/or pout.	___

_____ Sulking and pouting helped me get my way. _____
_____ Swearing was common in our house. _____
_____ We had many secrets from each other. _____
_____ Telling the truth was important. _____
_____ In an argument people sometimes hit each other. _____
_____ I sometimes hit people when I'm angry. _____
_____ Mom and dad often spoke the words "I love you" to me
        and others. _____
_____ My parents were openly affectionate with each other. _____
_____ Arguing was not permitted in my family. _____
_____ It's easier to show my love than to speak it directly. _____
_____ I find it difficult to confront issues directly. _____
_____ When you ask me what's wrong, I deny anything is wrong. _____
_____ The men in our family refuse to communicate. _____
_____ Women in our family manipulate others to get their way. _____

B. Of all the items listed above, which do you regard as the strongest points (best qualities) in your relationship right now? (Put a * next to your strong points.)

C. Of all the items listen above, which do you regard as the weakest points in your relationship right now? (Put an X next to the weak points of either you or your fiancé.)

D. What did your family do that you would least like to see repeated in your own marriage?

_____

_____

E. What did your family do that you would most like to see repeated in your own marriage?

_____

_____

F. What change can you make right now in order to communicate better with your fiancé?

_____

_____

G. What change would you like your fiancé to make in order to help you communicate better as a couple?

_____

H. I believe we should communicate deeply with each other _____
_____ (How frequently?)

I. The best time for us to communicate is

_____

_____

    As soon as your fiancé is done, share your answers with each other and discuss them in some detail. Take the time you need to fully explain yourself and to truly understand one another.

Exercise 2.3

Complete the following sentences, using only one word (you might wish to refer to the list of feeling-words below):

How do you feel right now?

I feel _____.

I am _____.

List of feeling-words:
happy, sad, bitter, bored, afraid, eager, nervous, anxious, hurt, sincere, delighted, excited, irritable, angry, joyful, tired.

Describe your feeling. How strong is it? (Use a scale of 1 to 10, where 1 is very weak and 10 is very strong.)

_____.

What are your thoughts about having this feeling right now?

I think _____.

I feel that _____.

Now share your responses with your future spouse for a few minutes.

Exercise 3.1

A. Check the main sources from which you received information about sex and sexuality while you were growing up:

___ My parents.	___ Through Scouts or other
___ Courses in school.	organizations.
___ Through my church.	___ Planned Parenthood.
___ Through scripture.	___ From my friends.
___ From watching TV,	___ From watching how my
movies, etc.	favorite stars live.
___ Teacher, counselor, etc.	___ Discussions with family doctor.
___ Older brothers and sisters.	___ Former boyfriend/girlfriend.
___ Locker room discussions.	

How has this influenced your behavior? _____

_____.

How would you like your own children to learn about sex and sexuality?

_____.

Why? _____

B. When it comes to discussing sex and sexuality, which of the following statements would best describe you? (You may check more than one statement.)

___ I am very comfortable discussing sex and sexuality with others.
___ I am comfortable discussing sex and sexuality with my partner.
___ I am eager to learn all I can.
___ I have reverence and awe for the gift of sexuality.
___ Sex is something private which good people don't discuss.
___ I am eager for our marriage to begin so we can explore this whole area more fully.
___ My attitudes may be warped, but I enjoy them.
___ I feel pressured by the whole issue.
___ I don't believe there's anything for me to learn.
___ I'd rather not talk about it.
___ I know I will never change my attitudes.
___ This is a very difficult area for me to talk about.
___ Other _____

Why? _____

C. When I hear the word "sex," I think of. . . (Check all that apply.)

___ Tenderness	___ Trust	___ Terror

___	Affection	___	Babies	___	Lust
___	Fear	___	Joy	___	Disgust
___	Sleep	___	Birth control	___	Cuddling
___	New techniques	___	Playfulness	___	Orgasm
___	Belonging	___	Faithfulness	___	Wonder
___	Commitment	___	Being used	___	God
___	Giving myself to you	___	Bad memories	___	Romance
___	Satisfaction	___	Dirty jokes	___	Marriage
___	Pornography	___	Communication	___	Reverence

D. In the home where I grew up, the sexual atmosphere was generally: (Check all that apply.)

___	Non-existent	___	Affectionate
___	Open and loving	___	Open but not loving
___	Trusting	___	Caring
___	Healthy	___	Unhealthy
___	Closed	___	Tense
___	Abusive	___	Free and easy
___	Other_____		

E. When we marry, the sexual atmosphere I would like to have between us in our home is:

_____

_____

Why? _____

[Discuss each set of answers with your fiancé. Focus not only on the answers, but on *why* your fiancé answered in that way. Really reach for understanding. Can you live with your fiancé's attitudes for the rest of your life? If change is needed, what change would you like to see take place?]

Exercise 3.2

Go through the list below and check all the statements with which you agree. Put a * next to all the statements with which you *strongly disagree*.

____   I believe sex must be spontaneous to be good.

____   We should set a romantic mood before we make love.

____   Having sex regularly is a duty.

____   Men enjoy sex more than women do.

____   It's the woman's duty to be responsible for birth control.

____   There's no sense in making love if we don't feel close.

____   Sex will never be an issue in our relationship.

____   It's not possible to go for a period of time without having sex with each other.

____   Sexual intercourse is not a subject nice people discuss.

____   Men can never have sex often enough.

____   If sex is to be good, we both should reach climax.

____   Sex makes a man feel "macho."

____   I think it's important to invite God to be a part of our sexual relationship.

____   The primary purpose of sex is to have children.

____   It's not important how frequently we make love.

____   Planning to make love can take all the joy out of it.

____   The man is basically in charge of the sexual relationship.

____   Married sex can never be as exciting as sex outside of marriage.

____   Men know more about sex than women do.

____   When we make love, it's best to focus on our own pleasure and not our spouse's.

____   I can say "no" to sex anytime I wish.

____   Having a good sexual relationship will keep us faithful to each other.

____   Sex with the same person all your life can get to be boring.

____   If we can't make love for some period of time due to pregnancy, illness, travel, military service, etc., I will remain faithful to you.

____   Pornographic films and magazines will help our sexual relationship.

____   Sex is not all that important to marriage.

____   My partner needs to change his/her attitudes about sex.

____   I believe we need outside help (counseling) in this area.

____   I'm afraid that previous experience will affect the way we relate to one another.

____   I would like to trust God with our family planning.

____   I can't believe God has any interest in our sexual relationship.

____   I would like you to give up pornography.

____   I would like you to trust me more in this area of our relationship.

When do we talk with each other about sex and sexuality? (Check all that apply.)

___ We seldom or never talk about it.
___ When a problem arises.
___ When I'm in a romantic mood.
___ When you're in a romantic mood.
___ When we feel trusting with one another.
___ When we want to change one another.
___ When we want to learn more about each other.
___ When we are frustrated with each other.
___ When we're arguing and want to hurt each other.
___ When we're looking forward to what it'll be like when we're married.
___ Other_____

What holds me back from talking more with you about our sexual relationship?

___ Fear of offending you.	___	Don't want to argue.
___ Fear of turning you on.	___	We have no time to talk.

___ It's not proper to talk about it.
___ We're usually too tired to talk.
___ We're too busy to talk.
___ I'm embarrassed to talk about it.
___ I don't want to rock the boat.
___ I figure we can work it all out later after we're married.
___ We discuss sex and sexuality regularly.
___ We have achieved perfect understanding and acceptance of one another's views.
___ I don't want to be criticized.
___ I sense you don't want to talk about it.
___ I'm afraid you'll ask me to change.
___ I'm uncomfortable with some of your attitudes but don't want to hurt you by bringing them up.
___ I don't see the need to talk.
___ I don't want you to know how ignorant I am about it.
___ Other_____

[Exchange your answers with your partner and go over them, one section at a time. Be sure to listen attentively to one another. Ask questions. Find out why your partner answered as he/she did. Make sure you really understand one another. If changes need to be made, make plans for how those changes will begin now before you are married. Include going for professional counseling.]

Exercise 3.3

Below are a number of possible attitudes about having a family. Put a check mark next to each statement which you believe describes your attitude.

_____ The commitment to marriage includes the decision to be open to new life. It's a decision I want to discuss now and regularly throughout our marriage.

_____ Any decision to postpone a family should be made only on a temporary basis. It should be a topic that can be reopened at any time by either of us.

_____ Sometimes when couples marry, they both plan to continue full-time with their careers. After the arrival of the first child, however, one of them may decide to remain at home. Sometimes the other partner then feels cheated because he/she was counting on the extra income. These are decisions we'll discuss often and seriously.

_____ I agree with the research that indicates children benefit greatly when they are cared for by their own parents.

_____ I view children as a burden who will cramp our lifestyle.

_____ Children are a gift from God, a special source of joy and delight. They are also a call to spiritual and emotional growth as we learn the true meaning of selflessness and giving of ourselves to others.

_____ A decision about the number of children we'll have should be thoughtfully and prayerfully considered.

_____ If we choose not to conceive a child at any particular point, it will be an occasion of regret for me.

_____ I do not plan to have children in this marriage.

_____ If we are unable to conceive our own children easily, I would go to extraordinary means to conceive a child.

_____ I would be willing to adopt a child.

_____ If we were to be infertile, I would be deeply upset.

Now share your responses with your partner and discuss them with each other.

When it comes to having babies, I am the type of person who would...(Check all that apply.)

_____ Want to have as many as possible.
_____ Be very nervous about the whole thing.
_____ Be concerned about our finances.
_____ Look forward to playing with them.
_____ Worry about who was going to take care of them.
_____ Plan the whole thing very carefully.
_____ Tell all my friends immediately.
_____ Trust God to be with us.
_____ Be horrified just thinking about it.

___ Take on a second job or work overtime to support them.
___ Start planning immediately for their college education.
___ Take one day at a time.
___ *Never* agree to an abortion.
___ Other_____

I think the ideal time for us to start a family is _____
_____

Now that I realize that we need both intimate conversation as well as sexual intimacy, I feel...
_____

How can I make my life a total "yes" to you?
_____
_____

When you have both finished writing your responses, read one another's answers and discuss them in some detail. Make sure you fully understand and *agree with* what your partner is saying to you. If it's not possible to reach agreement, you may want to discuss this issue further with your pastor.

Exercise 4.1

A. You have come to the church to witness your commitment to marry one another. Why have you chosen to have your wedding witnessed by the church? (Check all that apply.)

____   It's traditional in our family to "marry" in church.
____   I have a profound faith in God.
____   The church building provides a beautiful setting.
____   My mother/father want us to be married in church.
____   My fiancée's mother/father want us to be married in church.
____   This church was a compromise for both of us.
____   I grew up in this church/this denomination.
____   I have a strong sense of belonging to this church.
____   My fiancée wanted a church wedding.
____   It feels right to make a permanent commitment in the presence of God.
____   Other_____

(What other reasons would you add for why you have chosen a church wedding?)

B. When it comes to making a permanent lifelong commitment to love someone, I'm the kind of person who would say (Check YES or NO to each statement):

YES	NO	
___	___	This is an easy thing for me to do.
___	___	This really scares me.
___	___	I'll try this, but if it doesn't work, I want to get out of it.
___	___	I really want God to bless this commitment.
___	___	I'm putting all my trust in God to help us.
___	___	I hope I never have to work at this relationship.
___	___	If times get difficult between us, I'm willing to go for counseling.
___	___	I hope we always grow more and more in love and I'm willing to work hard to make that happen.
___	___	Enrichment programs for married couples might be something that would interest me.
___	___	This commitment applies now, but if I continue to grow and change, it may not apply in the future.
___	___	I'm not sure it's possible to love someone for a lifetime.
___	___	I'm willing to change my priorities in order to make our marriage work.
___	___	Other_____

(What other things would you say about your permanent commitment to one another?)

C. What do you hope to gain from the church community? (Check all that apply.)

___ Nothing, really.
___ We simply want to use the church and have a minister preside.
___ We belong to this community.
___ We would consider belonging to this community.
___ We live out of town, but this community represents our own community where we live.
___ The church community speaks to me of God's love for me/us.
___ The marriage covenant is a private commitment. The church community has nothing to do with it.
___ Other_____

(What additional expectations do you have for this faith community you have chosen for your wedding?)

[Share your answers with your fiancée. Make sure you understand clearly what the other person is saying. If the other person does not share your views on certain questions, find out why he/she chose that particular answer.]

Exercise 4.2

A. When you think of God, what images come to your mind? (Check all that apply.)

___	Wise old man.	___	Harsh judge.
___	Scorekeeper of good and evil.	___	A mother figure.
___	The ten commandments.	___	A father figure.
___	A being of total love.	___	Creator of all.

___ One who inspires love in me.
___ One who inspires fear in me.
___ I don't believe in God.
___ I've never really thought about God.
___ I'd like to know more about God.
___ Other_____

(In what other ways would you describe God or your relationship to him?)

B. The following are words that have sometimes been used to describe Jesus. How would you describe Jesus? (Check all that apply.)

___	Gentle	___	Kind
___	Compassionate	___	A healer
___	Our Savior	___	The crucified
___	Redeemer	___	Demanding
___	My personal Savior	___	A friend
___	A brother	___	A trouble-maker
___	The Messiah	___	A prophet
___	A stranger to me	___	Not important to me
___	Challenging	___	Teacher

___ I have a personal relationship with Jesus.
___ I don't feel close to Jesus.
___ I don't know much about Jesus or his teachings.
___ I want to know more about Jesus.
___ I don't believe in Jesus.
___ Other_____

(In what other ways would you describe Jesus or your relationship to him?)

C. The following is a list of religious attitudes and practices. Go through the list and check off all those that apply to you. Put a * next to those that are *most important* to you.

___ I believe going to church every Sunday is important for us.
___ I want to make God the center of our home and our love.
___ I believe it is important to have outward signs of our faith in our home

(a cross or other religious symbols). The most significant religious symbol to me is _____.

I would like to have this symbol in our home. ___ Yes ___ No

___ I believe it's important to pray every day.

___ I plan to pray every day.

___ I would like us to pray together.

How often? _____

___ I believe that if we say we love God, we must also keep his commands.

___ I believe in God, but I don't believe any particular religious practice is necessary.

___ I don't believe in God and don't intend to practice any religion.

___ I'm angry with God.

___ I enjoy spiritual reading (i.e. Christian books, magazines, journals, etc.).

___ I would like you to continue to practice your faith after we are married.

___ I would eventually like us to become members of the same faith community.

___ I believe all things are God's gifts to us.

___ I believe God knows and loves each of us intimately.

___ I believe knowing and understanding the Bible is important.

I would like to attend Bible study classes after we are married. ___ Yes ___ No

___ I find God's presence everywhere.

___ I believe God helped us find each other.

___ I believe God blesses our love.

___ As a child I studied religion.

___ I want our children to study religion.

___ I believe baptism is important.

___ I want our children to be baptized.

In what faith community? _____

___ I believe there is life after death.

___ I hope to spend eternity with God in heaven.

___ I don't believe in life after death.

___ I believe it is important to have friends with whom we can share our faith.

___ I believe that if we are really living our faith, we probably won't always fit in with what others are doing in our society.

___ I believe it is important to avoid doing things which may hurt someone else or myself.

___ I believe we are called to forgive those who hurt us.

___ I try to forgive everyone who has hurt me.

___ I believe God will help us overcome any temptations that would destroy our marriage.

___ I believe we can make God's love real to one another.

___ I believe we can help one another get to heaven.

___ I believe it is important to be involved in church activities beyond Sunday services.

___ I will teach our children to pray and pray with them.

___ I will respect your religious beliefs and encourage you to practice your faith.

___ I will help you find time to pray each day.

___ I am willing to continue to talk to you about our religious beliefs.

___ I am willing to respect any differences we may have in our beliefs.

___ I will avoid any sense of religious superiority over you.

[Share your answers with one another. Take your time and go over them carefully—listening with your heart. If you wish, begin your discussion with a prayer and invite God to be with you as you discuss this most intimate part of your lives together.]

Exercise 4.3

What beautiful qualities does your fiancé share in common with Jesus? How has your fiancé brought Jesus' love alive for you? Go through the list below and put a check mark next to all those qualities of love you have seen in your fiancé in the time you have known one another.

____ You have always stressed my good qualities. I always feel affirmed by you.

____ You are not critical or judgmental of me.

____ You have always been faithful to me.

____ You have made me your first priority.

____ You brag about me to others.

____ You are not constantly threatening to break up with me.

____ You are enthusiastic in your love for me.

____ You are willing to sit and talk with me—to share your views and ideas and to listen to mine.

____ You are willing to come to days such as this to work at deepening our relationship.

____ You are passionate in your love for me.

____ You are not afraid of intimacy.

____ You never hold a grudge or say, "I told you so."

____ You are quick to forgive me when I have offended you.

____ You have never hit me, insulted me, or called me names.

____ You encourage me to try new things, take new risks because you are at my side.

____ I always feel special when I'm around you.

____ You are very tender and concerned when I don't feel well, or I am upset about something.

Now go back through the list and put a * next to your partner's strongest quality.

What qualities of Jesus' love do you plan to bring to your beloved in your marriage? (Check all that apply.)

____ I will love you with a passionate, life-giving, and holy love.

____ I will be faithful to you not simply in sexual matters, but I will carry you in my mind and my heart wherever I go.

____ I will make you my first priority—ahead of my friends and even my family.

____ I will brag about your good qualities to others.

____ I will not criticize you to friends.

____ I will praise and affirm you so that you may grow in confidence and self-esteem.

____ I will never threaten you with divorce even when I'm very angry with you.

___ I will love you enthusiastically and show my love for you in all the big and little ways that make you happy.

___ I will work on our relationship every day of my life.

___ If our relationship becomes difficult, I will get counseling or look for help and encourage you to do the same.

___ When I have hurt you, I will ask for your forgiveness.

___ When you ask for forgiveness, I will always grant it to you.

___ As far as I am concerned, this marriage is forever.

___ I won't get into a pattern of blaming you when things go wrong.

___ I will work on keeping our love alive and passionate, just as Jesus was passionate in his love for us.

Go back through the list and put a * next to the quality you feel most strongly about developing.

Now write a love letter to your partner and include the following points:

1. Tell your partner of the most beautiful quality you see in him/her. Give some examples of when you have experienced that quality.
2. Write of the quality you plan to develop in your relationship after you are married. Be as specific as possible. Which quality will you develop? How will you do it? What changes are you willing to make in order to accomplish it? If you have time, you may write about more than one quality.
3. Close your love letter with words of love for your partner.

When you have both finished writing, share your responses with your partner.

Postponing a wedding is always considered a drastic alternative—so drastic that few people consider it. However there are times when postponement may be the kindest and most intelligent thing to do. Here are some ideas to keep in mind if you should be having any doubts at all about whether or not you should marry.

When Should You Consider Postponing the Wedding?

- If either of you is basically an unhappy person—and only you can make the other happy.
- If either of you drinks too much or gets drunk frequently.
- If friends and family, job or hobbies are a higher priority than you are to each other.
- If either of you takes drugs.
- If either of you feels forced into marriage.
- If either of you has serious psychological difficulties and refuses to get help.
- If either of you has serious doubts about marrying but believes in going ahead because you made a commitment to one another.
- If either of you is trying to escape an unhappy home or difficult living situation.
- If either of you is marrying for money or financial security.
- If either of you is rebounding from a previous relationship.
- If either of you is marrying to prove something to others.
- If either of you has doubts about marrying the other but is reluctant to start over with someone new.
- If either of you is afraid you'll never marry anyone if you pass up this opportunity.
- If either of you feels as if you're settling for someone less than you wanted.
- If either of you is marrying because you don't want to upset the other person or your families by postponing the wedding or breaking the engagement.
- If either of you simply believes that one or both of you is not ready for marriage.
- If either of you refuses to change and takes the position, "What you see is what you get."

Don't marry anyone to rescue him/her. If you love one another, get help first. Go for counseling or treatment. After treatment is successfully completed, plan your wedding.

If you are pregnant, and are getting married because of the pregnancy, consider postponing the wedding until several months after the baby is born. The best gift you can give your baby is parents who truly love each other and chose to be married because they wanted to be together forever. The decision to marry should be made in complete freedom. You never want to say to one another in the future, "I wouldn't have married you if it weren't for that kid!"

If you have been unable to communicate well today—if you refuse to listen to each other seriously or to speak honestly to each other—communications won't become easier over time, only more difficult. You may want to take advantage of a few sessions with a professional counselor to help you in your communication skills.

You are about to take one of the most important steps in your life—perhaps the most important step. You are choosing to make a lifelong commitment to one other person—a person who will be with you through all the seasons of your life, all the way until death.

The only reason to marry is because you have found the most wonderful person in the world for you. You are deeply, passionately in love and you cannot imagine life without one another. You have found someone you can grow and share with physically, mentally, and spiritually. You share an outlook on life that draws you closer together and to God. Life doesn't get any better than this! Go for it!